LANDMARKS

LANDMARKS

AN IGNATIAN JOURNEY

MARGARET SILF

with illustrations by ROY LOVATT

Foreword by
GERARD W. HUGHES

DARTON · LONGMAN + TODD

First published in 1998 by
Darton, Longman and Todd Ltd
1 Spencer Court
140–142 Wandsworth High Street
London SW18 4JJ

Reprinted 1999 (twice), 2000, 2002, 2003 and 2005

ISBN 0–232–52254–5

Designed and produced by Sandie Boccacci
using QuarkXPress on an Apple PowerMac 7500
Set in 11/14pt Bembo
Printed and bound in Great Britain by
Page Bros, Norwich, Norfolk

CONTENTS

FOREWORD

I know of no publishing house which has ever offered to reimburse a buyer who remains dissatisfied after reading one of its books. I think Darton, Longman and Todd could safely make the first such offer with *Landmarks*.

If asked, 'What is the subject that interests you most, and on which subject do you consider yourself most ignorant?', the true answer for all of us is 'Me'. If any readers recoil from this answer, they might ask themselves, 'Do my ears prick up if I pass a group of people and hear them mention my name?' 'Have I ever felt anxiety while awaiting the results of an examination, whether academic, medical, or for a job?' 'When looking at photographs, some of which include me, do I give equal attention to every photograph?' 'Do I spend as much time looking at other people as I spend looking at myself in a mirror?' 'Why this disproportionate interest in me if I really know myself?'

Landmarks looks at the most fundamental questions which concern every human being, whatever their race, culture, religion or state in life. 'Where are you?' 'How are you and why?' 'Who are you?' These fundamental questions were explored by St Ignatius Loyola, a sixteenth-century Basque, in his book *The Spiritual Exercises*, which offers methods of discovering for oneself the answer to these basic questions. A friend of Ignatius, Jerome Nadal, on being asked for whom the *Spiritual Exercises* were suited, answered, 'For Catholics, for Protestants and for pagans'! *Landmarks* is similarly suited.

I am very familiar with the *Spiritual Exercises*. Over-familiarity has not bred contempt, but it does tend to breed boredom with books on Ignatian spirituality. In reading *Landmarks*, I was never bored for a moment, but delighted in following Margaret Silf's journey of exploration today, using the landmarks which Ignatius offered four hundred years ago. They are landmarks, not pillars supporting an immoveable shelter in which all readers must find refuge. The book encourages further exploration and provides a variety of exercises at the end of each chapter, so that readers can discover for themselves.

Landmarks is lucidly written, down-to-earth, free of jargon, full of hope and encouragement, and includes imaginative and helpful illustrations. Ignatius wrote his *Exercises* as a way of helping us to see and find the will of God. Finding the will of God can sometimes feel, in the author's words, 'like playing darts on an invisible board'. In this book she helps us to find the will of God within our own hearts, a will which is never directed to only our individual benefit, but always to the well-being of all peoples and of all creation.

GERARD W. HUGHES
December 1997

PREFACE: The Salad Bowl

Not long ago I was invited to attend a friend's induction as vicar of his new parish. After the service his new parishioners had put on a marvellous feast in the church hall. The trestle tables were set out with all kinds of goodies. The congregation streamed out of the church and into the hall. The place became alive with conversation, and, as so often happens at these gatherings, within ten minutes the laden tables were almost bare ...

... Except for one large bowl of rice salad, which remained untouched in the middle of a long, empty table. I happened to notice this salad and my heart went out to the person who had probably spent hours preparing it and had brought it as a love-offering. How hurt and saddened that person must be feeling, I thought. And my second thought was 'Why has nobody eaten it? It looks so appetising and inviting!'

Then it became obvious why the salad stood deserted and untouched, after the feast was over. *There was no spoon.* The fact hit me like a sledge-hammer that night. I realised that the salad bowl was telling me something about the Church. It, too, is sometimes like a bowl of salad, full of what people are so longing to receive, so *hungry* for. But where is the spoon? Shall the treasure remain forever on display, the inaccessible centrepiece of an empty table? Do God's people really have the means to eat the food he prepares for them, or is it wrapped up in the cling-film of doctrine and set high on the top shelf of theology? And are they too well-trained to dare to mention the problem?

No-one can know the mind of God. Yet surely he, like us, is saddened and grieved when his hungry children stand empty-handed at his table because 'the Church' has provided no spoons for the salad. Let us not complain ... let us, rather, remember that *we* are 'the Church', and that it is up to *us*, his people, to make his feast accessible to all, in whatever ways open up to us.

I can add nothing to the salad. I venture only to offer a little spoon. And

I can do that only because others have been 'spoons' for me in my own hunger for the living bread. They have made it possible for me to share in the feast. I would like to thank them for this quiet ministry that they maybe didn't even realise they were engaged in . . .

I thank my cousin, Ralph Wells, who influenced my childhood more than he or I quite realised, by his steady, unshakeable, uncompromising faith. I thank Michael Paton who accompanied my adolescent awakening to a deepening of faith as he prepared me for Confirmation, and Madeleine, my friend who died at that time, aged fifteen, already a candle for God which time hasn't extinguished in my heart. And I thank my parents, Irene and Bernard Ashton, who gave me the gift of growing up in a home where there was love.

I thank Brian McClorry, who carried me home when I had wandered far from my own truth, and has remained my patient, gentle and challenging companion through the years that are leading from truth to freedom. I thank Gerry Hughes for walking with me through the journey of the *Exercises* and beyond, for his wisdom in words and his communion in silence, and for the sheer gift of his presence. I especially thank Brian and Gerry for all their help and encouragement during the evolution of this book, and for their tremendous support and facilitation of the ministry of lay spiritual companionship, which they have done so much, personally, to bring about.

I thank my husband, Klaus, for his support and encouragement as a fellow traveller, for his untiring energy in making possible the Quiet Days for which this material was written, and for his invaluable technical expertise when it comes to using computers and other mysterious machinery. And I thank my daughter, Kirstin, for keeping my heart in heaven and my feet firmly on the earth.

I thank Terry Biddington for drawing me, against my own reluctance, into the first (to my knowledge) Ignatian discovery group in North Staffordshire, and for guiding me into the ways of imaginative prayer.

I thank Roy Lovatt for translating my half-baked ideas into the beautiful illustrations that accompany the text, Peter McClure for adding the lettering so skillfully and Sarah John for her inspired cover design. And I thank Morag Reeve, Helen Porter and Allison Ward of Darton, Longman and Todd, who have made my first real venture into the world of books such a delight.

So many people have shared their own inner treasure with me and have thereby enriched me more than they can imagine. Most especially, I would like to thank the 'Patchworkers' of Stoke-on-Trent and the 'Landmarks' group at Keele, for whom this material was originally written. My special thanks go to Elizabeth McNulty, who brought the Patchworkers to birth and nurtured them to maturity, Kasha Lawler for her unfailing 'post-natal' support of the group, Michael Miners for his support of the Landmarks group in and around the Keele University Chaplaincy and Mervin Smith and Paul Davies for their support of the Patchworkers in their parishes.

Almost all the examples in the book are drawn from my own personal prayer. I would, however, like to acknowledge a debt of gratitude particularly to Elizabeth McNulty who opened up for me, and for many others, the insights on the nature of Sabbath-time in Chapter 1 and to Gerald O'Mahony who demonstrated so vividly the effects of 'facing the sun' in Chapter 4.

Finally my thanks go to all who have walked alongside me in retreats and at other significant times in my life and have opened my eyes to the possibility of 'living the Exercises', especially: Helen Bamber, Renate Düllmann, Teresa Foster, the late Arnold Freeman, the late Paul Glendinning, Damian Jackson, John Marbaix, Tom McGuinness, the late Donald Nicholl, Tom Shufflebottom, and, supremely, Brian and Gerry. I thank you, from my heart.

BEFORE YOU BEGIN

This book is a companion for your inner journey. Take it gently, and enjoy the landscape as you go. Don't rush at it like a fell-runner, intent on breaking the land speed record. The more you savour the journey, the more you will benefit from it.

Some people like to take their walks alone. If you are journeying alone with this book, take the walk in your own good time, stopping wherever you feel the urge to do so – feel the bark of the trees, dip your fingers in the stream, gaze at the sunset for as long as you wish. It will probably be unhelpful to try to journey through more than one chapter at a time, and you may find that it suits you better just to explore one small section. Pick and choose from the suggested exercises at the end of each chapter. Stay with any that appeal to you and leave alone those that don't. You can safely trust your own sense of inner resonance to show you what is for you and what is not. You may find that the material in the book can offer you spiritual companionship through a sustained, home-based, prayer journey, or retreat, within the context of your daily life.

A solitary journey can, however, become lonely and disheartening and can sometimes lose its bearings. You might find it very helpful to find a companion with whom you can share your experience from time to time – a trusted friend who is 'on your wavelength', perhaps, or even someone you do not, yet, know personally, but who is willing to walk alongside you as, together, you seek to discern where God is for you on your inner journey. To find a 'soul-friend' may seem a daunting task: my advice is to look around your own circle of friends and fellow believers to notice any among them who are clearly people of prayer themselves (it usually shows, if you are observant, and it may not be the people you would expect!), to approach such a person and explain, very simply, what you are looking for. They may be very happy to walk beside you themselves, or recommend someone else who could be the right companion for you.

Other people prefer to journey in groups. If you are using the book as the basis for a faith-sharing group you will find that each chapter will give you material for the equivalent of one full day of reflection, with time to follow up some of the suggested exercises in a prayerful atmosphere, and, optionally, to share your reactions and responses with other members of the group. The sharing of experiences between trusted friends in this way is perhaps the most valuable exercise of all. The facilitator should aim to ensure that everyone in the group has an opportunity to share, to the extent that they wish to share (no coercion, please!). And, it goes without saying, complete confidentiality within the group is an absolute must: this requirement needs to be made clear from the outset.

When sharing spiritual experience like this, simply allow each person to make their contribution, leaving a respectful few moments' silence between one contribution and the next. There should be no interruption or discussion (since this is a journey of the heart, not an exercise of the head), and no attempt to 'correct' anyone's views or to offer advice. The truth that underpins this kind of faith sharing is that each person's experience is wholly and unquestionably valid and is offered as a gift of trust to the others. The aim should be that each person comes away from the encounter with increased confidence in their own experience and a deepened sense of their own unique value before God and to their peers. Remember that, when we open our heart's experience to each other in trust, we are entering on holy ground, where there is no place for comment, criticism or correction, but only for a response of loving acceptance. On this holy ground, God-in-you is *listening* to God-in-the-other.

If you are using the material for shorter faith sharing meetings, you may prefer to use just one or two sections at a time. The chapters are subdivided into smaller sections, each with its own heading, to give you a guide. It will be helpful if participants have an opportunity to read the material for themselves, in advance of the group meeting, and perhaps to use it as a focus for personal prayer. The group leader should, ideally, be familiar with the whole book and have a sense of its shape and purpose, before beginning the programme, and could, usefully, evaluate the suggested exercises in advance with a view to recommending an approach to their use in the light of the needs of individual group members. One model is for a facilitator to introduce a summary of the material at each meeting, section by section or chapter by chapter, and then for participants to use it for personal reflection over the subsequent week, and to share their reflections at the start of the next meeting of the group.

It is important that the material should be used in the order given, since it follows the dynamic of the *Spiritual Exercises* and each chapter builds on the reader's familiarity with what has gone before. However, it is *not* a commentary on the *Spiritual Exercises*, much less a way of actually *making* the *Exercises*. Having said that, a number of the participants in the two pilot programmes have indeed gone on to make the full *Exercises* in daily life, under personal direction, and have found *Landmarks* to be a valuable preparation for this encounter. A national and international network of Ignatian faith sharing groups and Christian Life Communities exists to help people who wish to take their journey further in this particular way. Contact addresses are given below, if you would like more information.

You may like to structure your meetings around shared prayer, possibly with appropriate music. A few sources that we have found helpful in the pilot programmes are mentioned below. You will, of course, want to add your own choices. A few helpful book titles are also suggested, for recommended further reading.

If at all possible, encourage your group to be ecumenical. You will quickly discover, if you haven't already done so, that when people begin to share together the deeper reaches of their hearts' journeys, the denominational divisions fall away, without any compromise of the genuine variety of riches between different traditions. The truth unites, and this is a journey towards truth. You will discover this most fully if your group is non-denominational, and open to people who are not aligned to any established Church or tradition at all.

How many people make a group? Well, where there are two or three gathered, there is a group, and there is God among them. At the other end of the scale, you may find that if numbers go above twenty it would be wise to split into two or more smaller groups. If intimate faith sharing is central to your meetings, you may find that a maximum number of about six is more appropriate.

And where to meet? Do try to find a congenial space. Often it is good to meet in each other's homes where the group size permits. Church halls and school classrooms are not congenial on the whole, and tend to be loaded with denominational bias or negative memories. In Stoke-on-Trent we have been very fortunate in enjoying the hospitality of the local

Franciscan community for one of the groups, and we have met in our own home with the other. You may find that a local religious community would welcome your approaches.

Finally, on the practical side, do try to keep costs to an absolute minimum. The whole ethos of daily life faith sharing and spiritual journeying is that it should be freely accessible especially to those people who lack either the time, the money or the freedom of circumstances to make formal retreats. Freely you have received. Give as freely as you possibly can. Quiet days, or simply quiet hours, can be arranged in each other's homes at no more cost than a pot of tea and coffee. Encourage everyone to bring a contribution for a 'bring-and-share' lunch or supper and you will be surprised at what interesting meals come together, if you can wean people away from their own pack of sandwiches! If you use other premises, or invite outside speakers, simply ask each participant for a small contribution to make a donation to your hosts or to reimburse your guests' travelling expenses.

The two original (ecumenical) pilot groups still meet regularly in North Staffordshire, to share their journeys and also to become a resource for others in the area. The *Patchworkers* of Stoke-on-Trent, and the *Landmarks* group at Keele join me in praying for every blessing upon *your* journey.

Music for the journey:
Dana: 'The gift of love'; 'In the palm of his hand'
Bernadette Farrell: 'Christ be our life'; 'God beyond all names'
Carey Landrey: 'Abba, Father'; 'I will not forget you', vols. 1 and 2
Tom McGuinness: 'Winter Gifting'; 'Exultet'; 'All will be well'
Marilla Ness: 'He touched me'; 'Come back to me'; 'Heart of Love'; 'Abba
   My Father'
St Louis Jesuits: 'Earthen Vessels'
General/instrumental: For example, 'Praise him on the pan pipes' (Simon
   Bernard-Smith); 'Angel Voices', 'Songs of Zion' (Maurice Sklar); 'Songs
   of Taizé' (Kingsway); 'Soften my Heart' (Nick Fletcher; Classical Praise
   series)

Suggestions for further reading:
William Barry, *God and You* (Paulist Press, 1987); *What do I want in prayer?*
   (Paulist Press, 1994)

Charles Elliott, *Praying the Kingdom* (Darton, Longman and Todd, 1985)

Thomas H. Green, *Opening to God* (Ave Maria Press, 1982)

Margaret Hebblethwaite, *Finding God in All Things* (Fount, 1994); *Six New Gospels* (Geoffrey Chapman, 1994)

Gerard W. Hughes, *God of Surprises* (Darton, Longman and Todd, 1985); *God, Where Are You?* (Darton, Longman and Todd, 1997); *Oh God, Why?* (BRF, 1992)

William Johnston, *Being in Love* (Fount, 1989)

David Lonsdale, *Eyes to See, Ears to Hear* (Darton, Longman and Todd, 1990)

Anthony de Mello, *Sadhana: A Way to God* (Doubleday Image, 1978); *Awareness* (Fount, 1996)

Donald Nicholl, *Holiness* (Darton, Longman and Todd, 1992)

Philip Sheldrake, *Befriending Our Desires* (Darton, Longman and Todd, 1994)

Jean Vanier, *Our Journey Home* (Hodder and Stoughton, 1997)

❦

To make contact with an Ignatian network in your area:
Mr John McGlinchey
1st Floor
Champleys Mews
Market Place
Pickering
North Yorkshire YO18 7AE

To make contact with a local Christian Life Community (faith sharing group):
Ms Teresa House
Christian Life Community
St Joseph's
Watford Way
London NW4 4TY

MEET THE GUIDE

In my 'day job' I am writing a programmers' *Guide* on how to overcome the problems in computer date management when we cross the boundary into the next millennium. How come, then, that I am sitting here today reflecting on the ways in which the insights of a man who lived 450 years ago in a remote Basque village in Northern Spain affect the way in which we relate to God today, on the threshold of the twenty-first century? I sometimes think that my PC will give a little shudder of culture shock when I expect it to process my thoughts on the problems of 2-digit date notation and the search for my deepest desire in the same breath.

This 'coming together' of two worlds apparently so far removed from each other is perhaps, in itself, a pointer to some of the treasures that are ours today through the legacy of Ignatius Loyola and the Society of Jesus, which he founded. If we can imagine him browsing through this book, or sitting among us as we explore these questions together, he would quite likely be smiling to himself and muttering something about *finding God in all things*. He would find it completely normal, and healthy, that we should be searching to deepen our relationship with God in the midst of life as we really live it – up to our ears in work or lack of it, mortgages, children and mess. He would be delighted to find that most of us are lay people, as he was himself when he was making his own journey of discovery. He would surely welcome the fact that we come from many different Church traditions or even from none at all. And he would be more than tolerant of the chequered histories we may have behind us, remembering the excesses of his own mis-spent youth. Most of all, he would recognise the love of God that is burning inside each of us, that is leading us onwards continually, like a beacon, to deepen our relationship with him, because it would reflect the experience of Ignatius' own heart and the source of his prodigious energy.

So who is this man whose life and discoveries are still affecting our own journeys so fruitfully? Before we begin our journey proper, let's just indulge for a few minutes in a time shift that takes us back to the age when Europe was in a similar kind of between-age turmoil as the one we are experiencing now, on the edge of a new millennium. A new age that isn't just causing havoc to our computer systems, but also seems to be heralding the dawn of a heightened awareness in people everywhere (whether they call themselves 'religious' or not) that there is more to life than the mere management of our days in such a way as to achieve a degree of comfort and security in the shifting landscapes of our lives.

Inigo Lopez, as he was born, made his journey through life, and to God, just as the world was coming, painfully and violently, out of the Middle Ages. The mere facts of his life can be summed up in a few sentences; its content was to be infinitely more far-reaching. He was born in 1491, the youngest of a family of thirteen, in Loyola in the Basque region of Northern Spain. When he was fourteen he was sent away to train as a royal page to the King of Spain and was introduced to the ideals of chivalry and knightly service. As he grew older he developed a more than passing interest in women, both those far away, in his daydreams, and those who were temptingly accessible. The last thing on his mind, during these years, was his spiritual journey or the inner movements of his heart.

The story of his life swerved round a big bend when he was in his midtwenties. The favour that his employer, a man called Don Juan Velasquez, had enjoyed in the royal court, came to an abrupt end on the death of the King. As a result, Inigo himself was unemployed, and chastened by his experience of how quickly and easily the power of riches and influence can disappear. With a parting gift of a few hundred crowns and two horses, from the widow of his former employer, he had to set off into the unknown, and start again.

The next phase of his life was to be in the household of the Duke of Najera, who employed him as a 'gentleman-at-arms'. Inigo learned to use weapons, and to help put down rebellions. His military training, under the duke, brought him, four years later, to a place called Pamplona, where he commanded a company defending the fortress against a French invasion. The defence had become futile and defeat was a certainty, but Inigo was stubborn to the limits, and absolutely refused to surrender. The price of his resistance came in the form of a cannon ball, which shattered his leg and broke his right knee. His days as a soldier ended in a stretcher, being transported home, in agony and humiliation, across the mountains, to his family home in Loyola.

It must have seemed like the end of the line. And probably most of us can identify with that drained, empty feeling of being at the end of our dreams and our resources, or helpless in pain or immobility, either in body or in mind. We can perhaps imagine how it might have been for this young man, in the prime of his life, to lie a helpless invalid, racked by pain, with nothing but his broken dreams for company. And imagining is exactly what he did . . .

Having asked in vain for something lively to read, in the form of romantic novels, he had to make do with all that the castle could offer, which turned out to be a *Life of Christ* and *Lives of the Saints*. We can perhaps feel with this stricken and disgruntled patient, as he spent his time between reading and daydreaming of all that might have been, had his injury not robbed him, at a stroke, of both his future as a soldier, and his attractiveness to women.

Daydreaming . . . ! Ironic that this man whose military skills and leadership potential were so remarkable, should have come down to us, most powerfully, as a *daydreamer*. But Inigo's daydreams held a potent secret. They had, locked up inside them, the key to the gift of *discernment*. And how did Inigo discover for himself this key that was to open up a gold mine in his heart?

Well, as the tedious, pain-ridden days passed, he indulged in two kinds of dreaming. On the one hand he still dreamed of the battles he would command, the military glories he would achieve, the noble ladies he would woo and win. But they were the dreams of *what might have been*, and, though they raised his spirits for a short while as he enjoyed the fantasy, they left him, in the longer term, feeling flat and disconsolate.

On the other hand, fired by the books he had been given, he started to dream of a King whose service was potentially even more desirable than that of the King of Spain; he began to wonder how this Christ-King might be served; he began to dream of out-sainting the saints in this great new quest that might be worth spending his life for. They were still daydreams, but he noticed an important difference in their after-effects. These dreams left him feeling inspired, energised and eager. They were not about what might have been, but about something that still lay dormant in the depths of his own heart, like a seed that had been mysteriously germinated and was pushing its way to the surface of his life, through all this heavy soil of pain and disappointment. These were dreams that didn't go away.

It was into this realisation of the difference between day-dreams and God-dreams (as we might call them), that the gift of discernment was given to Inigo. It was there that he discovered what we might call the 'inner compass' of his heart that was able to reveal to him which movements within him were capable of engaging his deepest vital energy, and which were only leading to fleeting satisfactions, that left him unchanged and unfulfilled. As he lay there in his enforced stillness and solitude, he learned how to notice his moods and feelings and reactions, and to measure them against this unseen compass. In his inner silence, he listened, with fresh awareness, to an invitation coming from deep inside himself, to enlist in the adventure of the service of God.

Day-dreams   or God-dreams?

As he ventured more and more deeply into the stories that were inspiring his new kind of daydreaming, he was also finding a new way of exercising his imagination. He began to participate in 'the plot', and find himself present in imagination to the scenes and conversations and stories of the Gospels. It was the start, for him, of an adventure into imaginative prayer, which was to become a most powerful catalyst for the growth of his personal relationship with God, and a method of prayer that is just as vividly available to us today.

On his sick bed, therefore, Inigo had experienced deep conversion. Gradually, after many setbacks, he limped his way back to life. But it was never again to be the life that he had known before, and that the cannon ball had blown to pieces. Now Inigo was a pilgrim of God, to whom he was ready to offer all his ideals of knightly service and courage and persistence. The next step was to tell his family ... and, as for so many who have walked this path in their own personal ways since then (including, surely, many of you who are reading this book today), this wasn't easy! Against a backdrop of pressure to use his skills and gifts to bring honour to the family name and help maintain the family property, Inigo made his excuses and left ... neither he nor his family knowing with any certainty where he was heading, or towards what vision.

Inigo the nobleman, the soldier, the fearless defender of Pamplona, had become Inigo the pilgrim.

The first stage of the pilgrimage – that search for the 'I know not what' that was urging him onwards – took Inigo to the Abbey of Montserrat, high on a jagged mountain peak, overlooking the plain of Manresa. Here he desired to make a full confession of the sins of his earlier life, and to begin again. His confession is said to have taken all of three days to make, and he received absolution from one of the monks there. He exchanged his nobleman's dress for the simple outfit of a poor pilgrim, and made a night vigil of prayer. He gave his clothes to a beggar, and his mule to the monks, and left his sword and dagger behind as an offering at the altar and a sign that he had exchanged his life in the service of the world's values for one committed to the service of God.

As the new pilgrim made his way down the hill of Montserrat, to the plain below, his mind must have been full of the experience of his conversion, his confession, his vigil, and the advice he had been given by the monks on the life of prayer. To all this new experience, he surely applied the ways of discernment that he had discovered in his dreams at Loyola. He felt the need to stay awhile, in quiet, to reflect on all that had passed, and everything that God seemed to be showing him through it, and to make some notes on his reflections. And so it happened that, instead of going straight to Barcelona as he had intended, he settled in the nearby town of Manresa for 'a few days', which stretched into eleven months. In Manresa the next stage of his life took shape.

Determined to live true to all that he had promised God up in Montserrat, the proud and self-willed Inigo now faced a life of begging for his daily food, and submitting to the relentless mockery of street urchins, probably better dressed and cared for than he was himself. Living out, down on the plain, in the heat and the dust of everyday reality, the high dream of the mountain, proved to be, for him, as for us, a constant struggle. He treated himself harshly, but he never forgot the agony of his own long sickness in Loyola, and he turned that memory into service by trying to help the sick in the hospitals of Manresa. He prayed, until prayer became a part of his every waking moment. And at last he found a cave near the river where he made a 'desert home' for himself. That cave was to become a space where his love and his understanding of God was to deepen beyond anything he could have imagined, where he was to receive insights that remain fresh and valid for us today, and where, very importantly for us, he was to capture the fruits of his conversion, his prayer and his reflections in written form.

Perhaps inevitably, given what a good thing was gestating in his heart, Inigo also fell victim to the onslaught of negative movements, or the 'false spirits' as he would have called them. He suffered endless self-recrimination about his sins, real and imagined. He experienced dark depths of despair and came close to taking his own life. It was, perhaps, a black time, shot through with golden streaks of insight and passionate commitment to God; or it was a golden time of spiritual growing and maturing, shot through with the darkest shafts of doubt and despair. Either way of looking at it may find its parallels in our own experience of those times in our lives that are at once both fraught with struggle and alight with the flame of our desire to take hold of the vision of our hearts.

The fruit of Manresa was a man who had freely bound himself in joyful service to a King called Christ, and who had been so opened up to the inpouring of the Holy Spirit that he was gifted with the ability to interpret his own personal experience in a way that has universal validity and significance. The distillation of this experience and the wisdom that it engendered is recorded in an unassuming little book called *The Spiritual Exercises*. Inigo's notebook was to become a guide, based entirely on his own experience, on how to become increasingly sensitive to God's action in our lives, how to discover and live true to the very deepest desires within us, how to make decisions that reflect God's indwelling presence in the innermost freedom of our hearts, and how to engage our lives consciously with the life of Jesus, God-made-man, through the living spirit of the Gospels.

It would be nice to record that Inigo went from strength to strength in

Spiritual
Discovering who I really am
Directing myself towards
God
Noticing God's action in
my life
Responding to the
movements of my heart
Discovering the nature
of my deepest desire
Seeking God's will

Exercises
Becoming free of all that
distracts me from my deepest
desire.
Making choices in line with
my truest self
Connecting my lived experience
with the life, death and
resurrection of Christ
Responding to God's
love for me
Finding God in all things

his life of discipleship. Of course, it wasn't so. How could it be? We all know, too well, that things never are like that. His own dream of serving God in the Holy Land was dashed by an intractable veto from the authorities there. His travels were overtaken by ill-health and near shipwreck. His attempts to help others by sharing his *Exercises*, in 'spiritual conversations' collided with the opposition of the Church (which eventually subjected him to the Inquisition) and the secular authorities, who, among other things, threatened him with a public birching. Injustice, humiliation and betrayal became his familiar companions, but they were carrying a hidden gift: through them he came to realise that his desire to be where Christ is was stronger than his desire to avoid the indignities and disgraces that the world and the Church meted out to him.

Through all of this, a word that springs to mind, and that was to become a keyword in Inigo's life, is the word *'companion'*. Already in Manresa, Inigo had begun to share his experience with a few companions who showed interest in his *Exercises*. He used his own notes as a guide to help him to help them. And this continues to be the way in which the *Exercises* are used: as a guide to a director, or mentor, or soul-friend, in helping another person discover, in prayer and reflection, God's action in his or her life. They are a way of helping people to 'discover for themselves' where God is for them and where they feel called to be for him.

Inigo's ministry of companionship grew and strengthened when he became a student in Paris, belatedly trying to acquire the academic qualifications that would overcome the objections the Church raised against his speaking to others of spiritual matters without ecclesiastical authority. (He was eventually ordained in 1536, at the age of forty-five, and adopted the name Ignatius.) There, in Paris, he, and his friends Francis Xavier and Peter Favre, were to deepen their friendship into a bond which forged them into the first Jesuits, as together they formed the Society of Jesus. By 1534, this little group of companions had grown to seven, and on 15 August of that year they bound themselves into an embryonic religious order. On that day they shared the Eucharist together and made their vows, and then celebrated . . . with a picnic!

Over 450 years separate us now from that inconspicuous event on the outskirts of Paris. For the first seven Jesuits there was surely no sense of disconnection between the deep seriousness of their commitment to God and to each other, and the simple, exuberant joy of their celebratory picnic. Among the many riches that have come down to us from that small group of friends, we might perhaps focus on that 'coming together' of all that makes us human: our searching and desiring, our failing and falling and fun-loving, our shipwrecks and our picnics.

Just as my computer happily accepts all that comes, whether on ancient spiritualities or problems of binary notation, so our inner journeys, surely, are about *all* of us, just as we are, with no arbitrary demarcations between 'work' and 'prayer', between 'secular' and 'spiritual' or between God and 'real life'. Above all, perhaps, Ignatian spirituality is about finding God in our lived experience and allowing him to transform that experience, through his Spirit, for ourselves and for all the human family.

The explorations in this book, like Ignatius' own explorations, also began as a response to groups of friends who wanted to come together to share their search for God. And, like his, they, too, are carved out of personal experience – some of it joyful, some of it painful, all of it *lived*! They are offered in the spirit of Ignatius in the hope that they may provide a few landmarks in the mysterious and sometimes hazardous terrain of our hearts as we make the journey inwards towards the pearl of great price, that lies both at our own deepest centre and far beyond our wildest imaginings.

Landmarks help us to find our way on a journey, by giving us a *point of recognition*. We notice something we recognise – some feature of the landscape – and it *locates* our position: 'Yes – I recognise that! So I must be

somewhere around *there*.' They give us confidence that we are not completely lost. They help us to find our bearings and discern the direction for
the next stage of the journey. When we are in unfamiliar terrain (and life,
for all of us, from today onwards, *is* unfamiliar terrain!) landmarks help us
to find ourselves and encourage us to keep walking. Something outside
ourselves – something that everyone can see and recognise (even though
they may see it from a different perspective and give it a different name)
relates to precisely where we *are*. It places us, as individuals, within the
wider landscape.

Maps and guidebooks would do just as well, you might say. And when
it comes to the spiritual journey of our hearts, there is no shortage of maps
and guidebooks, ranging from the 'Go this way, or else!' variety of creed
and catechism, to the 'Fifty ways to climb the ladder of perfection' sort. The
thing they all have in common is that they can be read in an armchair.
They can all teach you how to swim without getting wet.

Landmarks won't let you do that. Landmarks are no use at all unless and
until you are on the road! They are effective only in that they *connect* where
you are, in your own lived experience, to a point of recognition and
orientation, for your own story and for the whole human story.

I remember smiling once over a particularly colourful description of a
walk by the late A. Wainwright in one of his mountain walks guides, which
included the bizarre instruction to 'turn left at the third hawthorn tree'.
This unlikely piece of wisdom made a gentle mockery of all the intricate-
ly drawn maps in the book. That third hawthorn tree just *had* to be
discovered. It was a clue on a treasure hunt, and it demanded not only that
I actually make the walk, but that I do it *now* (before the number and
arrangement of the hawthorn trees should change beyond recognition). It
was information distilled from his own walking of the path, and gladly,
exuberantly, shared with me, his reader and fellow-walker. The excitement
of his own discovery infected me with the desire to make my own. It felt
both personal and universal, rich with the paradox of a season ticket valid
only for the present moment.

Perhaps the landmarks in this book share something of the quality of
Wainwright's third hawthorn tree. You may recognise them, though you
might not call them by the names I know them by. I hope they might help
you find your own way to the greater and greater treasure beyond the
clues. But you won't find them until you take the risk of losing yourself,

by setting out, and by keeping going – and all in the timeless urgency of the present moment.

Landmarks are not for the 'pillars of the Church'. They are for the People of the Way.

1. WHERE AM I? HOW AM I? WHO AM I?

Before we begin to explore the particular ways in which Ignatian spirituality can help our inner journey, we need to take a look at our inner 'landscape', to establish our bearings and see where we actually are. This is really the purpose of this first chapter, and to help in this locating exercise I have used the picture of three concentric circles.

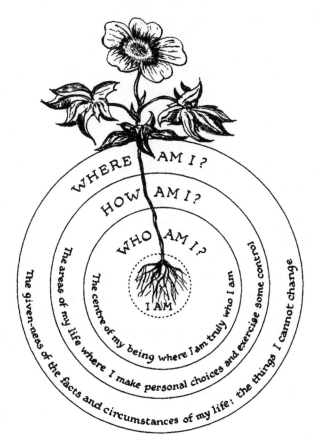

Let's begin the journey on the outermost perimeter. This is what I have called the WHERE circle. It represents all those things in my life that I cannot change: my natural family, my genetic makeup, the place and culture into which I was born, my upbringing, my education, all the things that have happened to me that make up my history, my natural giftedness and my inborn shortcomings, my health or my disabilities. These things form the given-ness of my life. They are the *facts* of my existence. They are, quite simply, WHERE I AM. Not only can I do nothing to change them, but they occupy almost all my consciousness and my energy. Whether I like it or not, I live here, on the outside edge of myself, for most of my waking hours.

Now let's move inwards to the second circle. I call this my HOW circle, because it is the area of my life where I can exercise some choice. In this area things happen to me, but I can choose how to respond to them. I can accept or reject, condone or confront, go with the flow or stand up to be counted. I can make personal relationships and take personal initiatives. Every minute that I live changes the kaleidoscope of events that bombard me, and every choice I make subtly, but certainly, goes towards making me HOW I AM. Choices turn into habits, and habits become character. And this process goes further than the boundaries of myself. My choices, my habits, my character make subtle, but certain, changes to the HOW of the whole human family. My choices for truth make the world more truthful. My betrayals of my own integrity undermine the integrity of all.

For many people the journey stops here. They live in a world where events happen to them, and they make choices about how to react to those events. A few take the risk of going, consciously, into the third circle, the circle of WHO.

When I move inwards towards the centre of myself, I move closer to the person I most truly am, before God. This is dangerous ground. As I begin to see who I am – truly and without protective masks – I may find serious discrepancies between the person who lives in the WHERE, and the person God created me to be, in my WHO. I will find shame, but I will also find glory. I will move closer to the God who dwells in my heart, and the encounter will challenge me in ways I cannot predict. This is the power of prayer. This is the risk of the inner journey.

Growing the Godseed

You will see that the circles in the illustration have sprouted leaves and flowers. I haven't just added these for decoration. My own experience tells me that when I make the journey inwards, or rather, when I allow God to penetrate my centre – what we commonly call our 'heart' – a powerful creative act takes place. I have called it the germination of my 'Godseed'.

What exactly is a Godseed and what causes it to germinate? Well, the picture below may help to show what I mean. As Christians we talk about God as being both *immanent* (present to us, individually and collectively, in our hearts and in our human experience) and *transcendent* (utterly beyond our reach or imagination, totally 'other' and without limits).

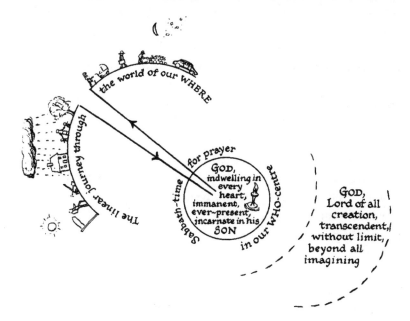

My Godseed, I believe, is nothing less than the immanent God locked up in my heart, and waiting to be set free in an act of germination, an act of resurrection. How does the germination happen? There are countless ways, and we can never pin God down by trying to define how God will act. One way of visualising this mystery is to notice moments when we seem to be in contact with something, or someone, beyond ourselves; it may feel like a tangent touching the outer circle of our lives. We know, at times like these, that something has happened that is different from the normal run of our daily lives, even though not separated from it. We might say that we feel as if we have been 'touched by God'. It could have happened in all sorts of ways – through a moment of intense communion with nature, or in a human relationship, a moment of deep insight that seemed to come from beyond ourselves, or perhaps a sudden clarity that showed us the way forward in a particular situation.

When these moments happen, we could say that God has not only 'touched' us but has somehow 'taken root' in our lived experience. That touch of Life will, if we allow it to, penetrate down through the layers of our experience, until it reaches the centre. There, the transcendent God who 'touched' us will join with the immanent God locked up, like a seed, in our hearts, and something new will grow from that union. The picture on page 31 shows the results. The flower (or plant or bush or tree!) will be the unique manifestation (or incarnation) of God that is ours, *and ours alone*, to bring forth. If we do not bring it to birth, it will not come to birth. It is the fulfilment of the union of our personal 'gene' with God. It is God's dream for us. It is the inner mystery of ourselves that is already known – has always been known – to God, that he is longing to bring to fulfilment.

This is an amazing and mind-blowing vocation for every believer. We might reflect, at this point, on Mary's response to the Annunciation, and take on board that moment in ourselves when God says: 'Are you willing to bring me to birth in your own life?', and our response is: 'Let it be done to me according to your will.'

Prayer as 'Sabbath time'

Suppose, then, that germination has happened. How can we bring God's dream to reality? I suggest that we can cooperate in this act, consciously and deliberately, in prayer. Prayer takes us to our WHO-centre. Through prayer we allow God to nourish our Godseed, and we ourselves are nourished by it. Jews, of course, have a very profound understanding of the word 'Sabbath'. For the Jew, the Sabbath is not for the sake of the weekdays; it is not an interlude for recreation to enable us to work all the harder during the week. Rather, the weekdays are for the sake of the Sabbath. The Sabbath is not just a break in the pattern of daily life, but the *whole meaning* of it.

In the same way, prayer is not just a means of sustaining us through our linear journey (though it does that too) but it is itself the reality of our journey; not primarily a calm interlude in our day, a 'quiet time', but the very essence of our being. When we are at prayer, we are most truly WHO WE ARE, and we are at prayer whenever we are really 'living true'. In later chapters we will look at how to recognise and foster this state of 'living true'.

... not just a linear journey through the days of our life

... but a radial journey into the deep heart of ourselves

... and then out again, bringing the seeds of transformation, out through our 'HOW' and into our 'WHERE'

It is in the light of this understanding of Sabbath that I have, in the picture on page 33, compared prayer to Sabbath-time. In one sense it is time taken out of our linear journey through our days. In another sense it is our most profound reality. When we pray, we move *inwards* to our God-centre. Then we move *out* again, back through the layers of our HOW, to our WHERE. This movement into the centre and out again is shown below. What happens at the centre is an act of *transformation*. Not that we come out of prayer transfigured, like Jesus on the mountain. Nothing so spectacular! Not a massive burst of radiation (which would surely kill us), but a subtle, gentle, perhaps almost indiscernible change in our way of being, that will carry its healing, changing power out through the layers of our lived experience, and infuse our WHERE with its Kingdom-values. This happens every time we pray, whether we are aware of it or not.

When we open ourselves to God in prayer, we invite him to enter our WHO centre, bringing the gifts of the Spirit into the heart of our lived experience, with all its problems, pain and sin. When he has done his transforming work, his Spirit in turn carries our needs and longings, and the needs and longings of all those for whom we pray, back to the heart of God. These are not just flights of wishful fancy. These are the promises he made to us, through his Son, and our lived experience testifies to their truth and their validity.

Before we leave the circles (and remember that they are only convenient images to try to capture something of what it is to be a believing human being), you may like to look at a few variations on what it might mean in other contexts to 'deepen' our perception of things from the outermost, surface level of response, to the deepest responses in the centre of ourselves, such as:

- The deepening of mere pleasure and pain through happiness and unhappiness, to joy and sorrow.
- The deepening of prayer itself from vocal or liturgical prayer through personal confession and meditation, to contemplative union with God.
- The passage from the transience of mere *feelings*, through the fidelity of *faith*, to the *fact* of God's unchanging love.
- The movement from being a person to whom things happen, through the realisation that we can influence what happens, to the acceptance of personal responsibility for being an event who happens to others.

- The movement from obsession with our immediate wants and fears, through the acceptance of responsibility in community and relationship, to the intimacy and trust of non-possessive love.

In each of these contexts (and I'm sure you can think of many more), you will notice an outer layer that could be compared to the WHERE experience, a deeper layer corresponding to the HOW response, and an innermost centre accessible only to our WHO reality.

This deepening, from WHERE, through HOW, to WHO is the hallmark of all personal prayer – perhaps especially so in the Ignatian tradition, which encourages us to begin by finding God in the ordinary 'outward' things of our lived experience, and allowing that discovery to draw us down to his deepest meanings for our life and growth in him.

The 'weeks' of our heart

In his *Exercises*, Ignatius invites the pilgrim to follow a framework of prayer which he divides into four 'weeks'. These are not weeks of the seven-day variety, and are not intended to map onto calendar weeks. Rather, they are 'phases' or stages through which the pray-er will move, as he follows this framework, and everyone who 'completes' the *Exercises* realises that 'in the end is the beginning'. A person coming to the end of the 'Fourth Week' prayer may well discover, for example, that she is frequently re-connecting to the prayer of the First Week.

Perhaps this is one of the hidden graces of the *Exercises*, that we get in touch with these many different 'weeks' within ourselves, and in the inner movements of our hearts, and that we come to realise their total *interconnectedness*. We don't have to progress neatly and tidily from fallenness to resurrection, in our life with God. The pattern of redemption isn't a straight line, or even a wavy line. It isn't even a circle, because each time we re-connect to our 'beginnings', the connection is different, and the circle is re-drawn in a new and different way.

This pattern, which sounds so mysterious when we attempt to describe it in words, is actually as simple, and as beautiful, as the earth itself.

On the surface, and above, there is the weather, constantly changing, yet each kind of weather bearing its own gifts – some welcome, some less so. Sometimes the weather is extreme and 'out of order', sometimes it is moderated and balanced. In its unreliability it feels just like us, and our moods and feelings.

Then there is the layer of topsoil, just underneath our 'weather' and very much influenced by it, but more stable, and carrying the Godseed for germination and growth. This is our heart-soil where God is growing his Kingdom.

And under the soil, the bedrock. Whenever we go deep, in prayer, or in relationship with God and with each other, or into the mystery and meaning of things, we will eventually come up against this hard rock. It can feel like the solid door of a locked room. There is no way out: no way in. So dark it is, that we don't even rightly know whether we are trying to get *in* (to a treasure chamber), or *out* (of a prison cell). Maybe both. Yet God is the bedrock, just as he is in our weather and our soil. The rock is his unwavering holding of us, the solid foundation without which we would sink into the quicksand. But it is also the hard rock that shatters us when we fall upon it, and which breaks us open, as it broke God himself upon the cross.

And because that rock opens up, from time to time, in our inner vision —

... the weather, the soil, the rock and the fire ~ images of the four 'weeks' of the Exercises.

glimpse-wise and terrifyingly – as it did when Jesus uttered 'It is completed!', and as it does for us sometimes in the dreadful movements of our inner earthquakes, or in silent, secret shafts of burning light that occasionally streak through prayer or dream – because of these we know that beneath the bedrock is an ever-blazing fire. This feels like the molten centre of ourselves, the source of our passion and energy. Like our surface weather, it is sometimes wild and disordered, sometimes creative and life-giving. This same inner fire is also the fire of God at the heart of all his creation. Sometimes we dread it, because it has the aspect of the flames of hell. Sometimes we long for it, because it seems to be alight with the very splendour of God's eternal presence and the radiance of heaven. This same fire, surely, licks our own hearts too, sometimes rising to reproach and consume us, sometimes seeming to transfigure us and our whole view of the world.

These four layers: the weather, the soil, the rock and the fire are also vivid images of the four 'weeks' of the Exercises:

- The weather of ourselves, our moods and feelings, our dependency on God, our transience, our unreliability, our fragmented nature, now rain, now sunshine, storm and glory. Insubstantial in itself, yet *affected* by the deepest movements of our heart, and *affecting* every other creature on the Earth. The brokenness of sin, spanned by the rainbow of an unconditional love . . . the *First Week*.
- Then the soil of our growing, learning, listening, sitting at the feet of the Lord, imbibing his goodness; sharing in his earthly ministry; becoming, in him, the person we truly are; taking root, following our deepest desire, striving up to the light, being pruned and tended . . . the *Second Week*.
- Then the splintering, shattering rock. The breaking open and the breaking down. The Calvary journey, with the Lord and in ourselves . . . the *Third Week*.
- And then, the earthquake of 'It is completed!' Earth splits open and its heart-fire flows free. Consuming and destroying, or quickening and energising. Destroying all that is not Truth, and transcending truth into Life. The fire of the Spirit, breaking open the locked space of the tomb . . . the *Fourth Week*.

And in the end is the beginning. The explosion of resurrection energy at the heart of things changes the surface weather for ever, and the weather affects the soil, and the roots of our Godseed touch the bedrock of God's love, and the cycle continues, but always differently, always uniquely. And when all cycles are fulfilled, the Kingdom *is*.

The search for freedom

Finally, a word about freedom. We will be looking at what 'inner freedom' might mean in more depth in a later chapter. However, while we are with the circles, it is worth noticing what inner freedom does, and does not, mean, in terms of our journey to the WHO centre.

The temptation is to seek 'freedom' by moving from one spot on the WHERE circle to another, as the picture shows. I would be free (and, therefore, fulfilled and happy) if I were not in this place (in this relationship, in this job, etc.) and so I will seize my 'freedom' by moving. What happens, if we do this, is that we exchange one unfreedom for another. We uproot our Godplant and expect it to flourish better elsewhere.

A second possibility is to move not sideways, but inwards, into the WHO centre, taking all the pain of our unfreedom with us, and allowing ourselves to be 'dipped in God' (as D. H. Lawrence describes it). Then we will return to the same place on our WHERE circle, but in a transformed way (however slightly). The result will be to make that part of our WHERE a little bit more free.

This is not to deny that a change of circumstances can sometimes be necessary and beneficial. But it *is* to say that real and permanent change and transformation happens in the WHO and not in the WHERE of ourselves. Changing the WHERE may well free us *from* something that we find oppressive or destructive, and sometimes that may be a necessary stage in our journey. But the deepest purpose of transformation is to free us *for* something, and that 'something' is nothing less than the coming of the Kingdom, our own personal resurrection, and the resurrection of the whole human family.

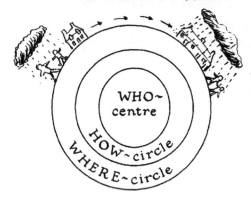

FREEDOM happens

not by moving
from one spot on
the WHERE~circle
to another...

...but by moving
into the WHO~centre,
in God's presence,
and allowing
ourselves to be
'dipped in God', then
returning to the
WHERE in a transformed
way, to make that part
of our WHERE a little
bit more free.

1: WHERE AM I? HOW AM I? WHO AM I?
Suggestions for prayer and reflection

In the sixth month the angel Gabriel was sent by God to a town in Galilee called Nazareth, to a virgin betrothed to a man named Joseph, of the House of David; and the virgin's name was Mary. He went in and said to her, 'Rejoice, so highly favoured! The Lord is with you.' She was deeply disturbed by these words and asked herself what this greeting could mean, but the angel said to her, 'Mary, do not be afraid; you have won God's favour. Listen! You are to conceive and bear a son, and you must name him Jesus. He will be great and will be called Son of the Most

High. The Lord God will give him the throne of his ancestor David; he will rule over the House of Jacob for ever and his reign will have no end.'

Mary said to the angel, 'But how can this come about, since I am a virgin?' 'The Holy Spirit will come upon you,' the angel answered, 'and the power of the Most High will cover you with its shadow. And so the child will be holy and will be called Son of God. Know this too: your kinswoman Elizabeth has, in her old age, herself conceived a son, and she whom people called barren is now in her sixth month, for nothing is impossible to God.'

'I am the handmaid of the Lord,' said Mary, 'let what you have said be done to me.' And the angel left her.

(Luke 1:26–38)

Try to imagine yourself as part of this scene. Paint a picture in your mind of the surroundings, the houses, the fields, the village, the weather, the sights and sounds and smells of the place. Are you a bystander, or alongside Mary, or are you alone there?

Imagine the arrival of the angel. Hear his words. Notice your reaction. Ask God to open your heart to hear and understand anything God may wish to reveal to *you*, personally, in this scene. Be still, and let his meanings arise, unobstructed, to your consciousness and respond to them in whatever way feels right for you.

❦

Use a sheet of blank concentric circles and fill in anything you find helpful to you about your own personal WHERE-circumstances, or about the way your HOW-circle is forming as a result of the decisions you have made in your life. Make a note of those things you cannot change and face your feelings about them. Look back over the past day, or perhaps the past week, and recall any moments of decision. How did you react to them? Where do you feel that your choices were made in a you-centred way, and where were they God-centred? How do you feel about them now? You may like to tell God, in prayer, how you feel about them and show God anything you would like to change.

❦

Recall any events or relationships in your life when you have tried, or wanted, to achieve 'freedom' by moving to a different point on the WHERE-circle. Did you find the freedom you were seeking? Do you recall any times when you have stayed in a difficult situation, perhaps feeling imprisoned? How did you respond to that situation at the time? Would you react differently now? Bring your memories, including any regrets, to God and show him, without fear, how you are feeling. Ask him confidently for healing and for the freedom you are seeking.

※

Use the first picture in this chapter to reflect on God's dream for you, the fruit of your Godseed, which is rooted in your relationship with him, in your WHO-centre, but blossoms and bears fruit in the WHERE of your life. Let yourself be, in imagination, the flower (or plant or tree) that you are becoming. Now let yourself be in the roots. Feel them pushing down, deeper and deeper, towards the ground water and God. Feel the sap rising through you, thrusting its way to fulfilment.

※

Can you recall any moments when you have felt 'touched by God', in the kind of way that has brought your Godseed to life? Remember these moments now in prayer and thank God for them. Ask him to show you how they have indeed been bringing about the fulfilment of his dream for you.

2. ELEVEN TEAMS OF OXEN

The story is told in the Old Testament (1 Kings 19) of how the prophet Elijah called Elisha to be his successor. Elisha's response seems ambivalent: he wants to follow, but he also wants to say goodbye to his family. Eventually, after some hesitation, Elisha takes the step of commitment, accepts the mantle of prophecy from Elijah, and follows.

A companion, who was accompanying me for a while on my faith journey, suggested this passage as a scriptural focus for my own prayer one day during a retreat. I have no doubt, with hindsight, that he was expecting the Lord to touch my heart, through this passage, into a less ambivalent kind of discipleship for myself. In fact, however, the passage affected me in a quite different way, which took both of us by surprise.

My attention was captured by the picture of the eleven teams of oxen, ploughing the field ahead of Elisha, who was ploughing with the twelfth and final team in the line. I knew that this picture had touched on something at a deeper level than my conscious thought, so I stayed with it and let it form my prayer that day. I noticed that it released a deep feeling of peace within me, as if I had recognised something important there. It seemed to speak to me of a 'calling' that was not simply about my own response to God, but about the whole continuum of human response to the divine. Specifically, it seemed to be a call to me to recognise those particular 'oxen teams' who provided the guidance and the pulling power for me in the ploughing of my life's furrow: those men and women who were personal beacons for me on my journey of faith.

You might like to join me, retrospectively, in my meditation ...

Begin by imagining yourself standing outside your own home, beneath a brilliant starry sky. Take in the splendour and the immense space stretching out above you. Beyond our grasp. Beyond measurement. Out of reach. Utterly transcendent. An image of the infinite, yet connected to us as surely as we are connected to every other created thing.

Now see the constellations. Out of the infinity, there is something recognisable. You can locate yourself by it. It pinpoints you exactly at your own moment in time and space. Feel the thrill of being located at your own unique place in this immensity. Feel the thrill of claiming your place within the vast heart of God.

Now hear the word of Scripture. Elijah is calling Elisha to the life of a prophet of the Lord ...

> *Elijah left and found Elisha ploughing with a team of oxen. There were eleven teams ahead of him, and he was ploughing with the last one. Elijah took off his cloak and put it on Elisha.* (1 Kings 19:19)

Imagine yourself in a field. The field is being ploughed and you have your own furrow to plough. The field is the field of the world, where you are ploughing the furrow of your life. Your hands are on the plough, and your feet are heavy with the earth. Perhaps you feel that you are carrying out this gigantic task all alone. But look ahead of you. See the eleven teams of oxen that Elisha saw. You are not alone. You are part of a long line of life and of meaning. But this is not just any line of oxen teams. This is your own personal line, ploughing your particular furrow.

Who, or what, is in your line of oxen teams? Think of significant people who have made an important difference to your life. Some of them may be among the first disciples and saints. Some may be in your recent past. Some may be walking alongside you today. These are people who have helped to form the line of your life, your furrow. They have helped to provide the pulling power for your plough. And they have helped to guide its progress.

Not just people, but important moments, events, decisions or experiences will have formed your furrow. Remember them. See how they have moved you on, or possibly corrected your direction.

Notice the landscape of your part of the field. The places that have been important to you.

If you ask a farmer how he ensures that he is ploughing a straight furrow, he will give you this advice: Fix your eyes straight ahead, on some fixed point on the horizon – a tree perhaps – and keep moving steadily towards it. Don't watch the furrow. Just keep your hands on the plough and your eyes on that fixed point.

Jesus is our fixed point. He is at the head of each one of our personal lines of oxen teams. It is his risen life and energy that provides the power for our every movement. But he gives us, too, our own personal constellation of people (past and present), and landmarks and signposts for our unique journey.

Hands
on the
plough,

eyes
on the
destination

Let your journey bring you back to your place beneath the stars. Remember your line of earthly oxen teams and see them as a reflection of God's personal shaping of your life, mapped out in the infinity of his heart.

Like the stars, they can locate you firmly on the solid ground of your own life, and they can reveal much to you about your journey. They can help you find your way. They can be channels to you of that driving energy of the risen Christ who is always your pulling power and your destination.

When you look back over the line of people and events that have shaped your life, you are also looking forward to your destination, because Christ is truly the beginning and the end, the alpha and omega of your own being.

Gently return to your place in the here and now, strong in the knowledge that you do not plough the field alone, and that the story of your life will lead you back through your special landmarks to the Lord himself, the Lord of your harvest.

The River Mee

If you are not moved to plough fields, you might find a gentler image more helpful. Perhaps you might reflect on your life as resembling the flow of a river, from its first beginnings in a hidden, secret source, to its outflowing into the ocean of its destination.

I remember a marvellous weekend I once spent with relatives in Scotland. They had just moved to a new home in the Scottish Borders. On the Saturday they took us out for a drive to show us their new surroundings, and we came across a sign that marked the source of a river – that elusive, indefinable point where the waters gather and a New Thing begins. 'This is the source of the River Tweed', the sign read. I'd never seen such a sign before – probably because it is extraordinarily difficult to locate exactly where a river has its source – just as it is difficult to define exactly when a new human life begins. For a river, as for an embryo, there is that vague, invisible time of not-quite-thereness, where waters are gathering, cells are multiplying and there is a hint of something – someone – new that may, or may not, come to fulfilment.

Anyway, our little outing that day seemed, from then on, to be defined by that chance meeting with the sign marking the river's source. In the speed and comfort of the car we travelled in minutes a journey of forever, from the ever-springing, never-quite-discernible source, down the trickling burn, along the gathering river. In minutes, the almost-nothing source was a river where fishermen sat, dipping their boots into trout-fertile waters, where trees sprang and rooted, giving leaf-cover, shade and fruit in due season. In minutes the hidden source had become a stately presence in the valley town, spanned by a proud, wide bridge, humming with Saturday people and the plaintive song of the bagpipes.

In minutes, from the wild unknown of a secret source, to the tamed and admired, that could be named, and lived alongside, fished and bridged and celebrated, before it spilled itself again into the boundless, unnamed and unnameable ocean. The telescoped adventure of a forever-journey.

For the River Tweed, you might like to substitute the River Mee, and reflect on the course of your personal river so far (like the meanderings in the picture), and on where you think, or hope, or dream, that it might be leading.

The river makes a difference to the landscape through which it flows. It carves its way through the earth – hard clay or soft sand – where it finds itself; it finds ways to go beyond the obstructions and blockages that it meets; it may flow underground, forming channels and caves, or it may spread out and water the land around it. And the relationship is mutual, because the landscape makes a difference to how the river flows and where its destination is to be. The landscape gives the contours that determine the water's journey; it offers space for the flow, or resistance; it cooperates with the power of the water, or it struggles against it.

This is only a metaphor, of course, but you may find that some reflection on the relationship of your own life's river with its given landscape reveals much about who you really are, what influences are forming you, what you welcome in your story and what you fight against, and above all, what you dream of becoming as you widen and deepen towards your destination. This is the landscape of your circumstances, your origins, your family and friends, those people who have been important in your life, those events that have pointed out new directions to you, the difficulties you have had to negotiate and those aspects of the scene that have given you energy and joy.

Like my drive along the River Tweed, your reflections may cover in minutes what has been evolving since the moment you were conceived. And conversely, they may lend timeless significance to the passing

A child is born...
the flow of my life begins.

My source: in what space does my
life's flow begin? What gifts spring
up in me?

My tributaries:
who and what has
formed me into who
I am.

The river seems to
disappear underground.
I seem to forget
my deepest
desires.

The river runs
peacefully.

The river is diverted for
other people's purposes.
I feel exploited.

The river makes
detours. I am
straying from myself.

The river struggles through
obstructions, boulders,
dams.

The river dries up.
My life feels wasted.

The river hits rapids.
I feel frightened and alone.

The river runs
into bog-land and gets
stagnant. Maybe there
never was a flow.

The river widens
and deepens,
becomes a
source of
refreshment
for others,
flows into
deserts, making
them fertile.

Where is the
river's destination?

My deepest
desire ...?

moments of your daily life, if you flow on with open eyes ...

Consider, for example:

- What do you know, and value, of your own origins?
- What kind of landscape has your river flowed through so far?
- What kind of obstructions or hazards has it had to negotiate?
- Have you ever felt that your river's energy and power was being sapped and exploited by others?
- Has your life-river ever appeared to disappear? To go underground, or to dry up? To lose itself in the boglands or marshes of your experience?

- What detours do you see, with hindsight, that your life has made?
- How, and where, do you feel that your river is flowing *now*?

As you let your mind wander back along the river banks you have known, what landmarks make you feel glad and grateful? Perhaps particular people or experiences? Have you ever told those concerned what a difference they made to your journey?

What landmarks have left you feeling angry, or disappointed, misled, betrayed or in any way negative? If other people were involved in these situations in your life, do you still harbour resentments against them, or can you now turn round to focus on the future rather than the past? Are there things you would like to talk over with the people concerned? Do you feel able to do so? (Only do so if you really feel comfortable about it!)

Your faith story

A Faith Story (or Faith Biography) is simply an account of your inner journey through the outer events of your life; the story of how you have gradually (or suddenly) become aware of a relationship with God and the ways in which he has been leading you; a kind of inner map of the feelings life has roused in you, the decisions you have made along the way and the way you have made them, significant landmarks along the way when you felt that something 'grew' inside you, significant people who have walked alongside you at different stages of your journey and brought you closer to an understanding of yourself.

Why is it helpful to produce a Faith Story? There are a number of reasons:

- To help you to get in touch with the most important movements, events, people of your life and to notice the inner movements that reveal how God is touching your life.
- To draw together your life and your prayer, to help you to see every event and feeling of your lived experience as an invitation to deepen your relationship with God.
- To help you say to God: 'Here I am. This is how I feel I have become who I am. Let us journey on together towards who I shall become, in you.'

And how to do it . . . ?

One way to approach your faith story might be through one of the pictures we have looked at: the eleven teams of oxen, or the River Mee. Your faith story would be simply an expression of what those pictures have revealed to you.

This isn't a literary exercise. Your faith history is a very personal conversation between you and God. If you find it easy to write, you might like to write it out, perhaps in the form of an account of those events and moments in your life that were charged with special feelings – good or bad – for you. Or you may prefer to use drawings or symbols to express those things that have been important to you; some people find it helpful to use different colours to express their emotions with regard to these events.

It doesn't matter at all how you express your story. What is important is for you to get in touch with the movements in your life and in your feelings about your life, and by doing this, to get in touch with the ways in which God has been present to you in it.

Your faith story is yours alone. However, you may wish to share it, in part at least, with someone you trust and feel comfortable with. (The Celts had a word for such a person: they called him or her an *anmchara*, meaning 'soul-friend') To share your story in this way can help you to recognise the patterns and movements that it reveals, which in turn can help you to discern the ways in which God is present to your ongoing journey.

When you have expressed your story, as you see it now, keep it in a safe place, without changing anything. From time to time go back to it and see for yourself how it has moved on, which patterns and movements have become stronger, and how you feel then about the areas of light and darkness, the 'joyful' and the 'sorrowful' mysteries of your life. You may find that some of the sorrowful mysteries were in fact the places and the times when God was drawing you closer to him, drawing you into his own suffering, into partnership with the cross, or inviting you to grow beyond the hurts that hold you to the past.

And lastly, *enjoy* the exercise. Let your joys be joys and let your sorrows be brought into a healing light.

The end of the furrow

I have lived with the reality of my eleven teams of oxen for several years now, since the picture first suggested itself to me. But today I feel I know something of its ending. Even as I write, a dear friend is standing on the brink of death, surrounded by his wife and family. There may be a call at any minute to say that he has left us.

It's the first of May, and the world is simply burgeoning with springtime. Everywhere the blossom hangs so rich and heavy on the trees that you can almost taste the cherries. The oak trees are leafing early this year, and life is bursting its seams. It is also the feast day of St Joseph, the worker and faithful husband, 'God's foster-father', and my friend has been like a father to me – a spiritual father.

Here in Britain it is the day of the general election, a day that the politicians have called a day of destiny for Britain, and a day when many are hoping for a new start, under a new government, with a new vision of peace and social justice – a vision that was part of my friend's driving inspiration. This is a day full of promise and hope, but my heart aches for my dying friend. Yet he has lived a long and deeply fruitful life, and my tears are charged with the knowledge that what he has given me, and so many others, is not for grieving over, or even for holding onto, but for living out and for handing on.

He is one of my oxen teams. He has walked ahead of me in the field, showing the straight furrow, drawing me by the power of his own faith and urging me to 'keep going' and to keep my gaze focused on that fixed point on the horizon which marks the heart of our destination. Very soon he will become part of that destination. I thank him, even as I weep.

When Elijah came to the end of his furrow, he was taken up into heaven in a whirlwind. Elisha was told that if he was to continue ploughing faithfully in the spirit of the one who had gone before, and to receive the flame from the one who had run the race ahead of him, he must have the courage to watch, steadily, as Elijah was taken up to heaven.

When I first came across this story, I took it to be simply the dramatic account of an exceptionally charismatic prophet. Now I feel sure that it is a call to all of us. We all have our line of oxen teams. I hope that in this chapter you will have been able to get in touch with some of your own. We all draw energy and guidance from the personal 'wisdom figures' who have ploughed ahead of us along our personal furrow. We are all called to watch steadily, just as a relay runner watches carefully the approach of the one who will hand the baton to him to carry forward, or as an Olympic torchbearer watches as his turn approaches, to carry the flame onwards for the next lap of the journey home. If we watch steadily, we will plough sure and straight, and the energy of love and life and wisdom that has guided us, will pass in some way into, and through, our own hearts. It is given to us not just for our own sake, but also for the sake of those who will follow after.

❧

My friend has died now. He doesn't teach any more – he *is*. And that, surely is how God teaches us, by *Being*. Perhaps this change, when it starts to happen in ourselves, marks the transition from disciple to apostle – from one who listens and learns, to one who turns what is being learned into what is being lived. This happens when you, once the twelfth in your line of oxen teams, find that the baton has passed on to you, and that you yourself are being asked to take on your share of responsibility for providing the guiding and transmitting the pulling power to the ones who follow after.

And so I commend to you the task of discerning your faith story, for it is a sacred task. Learn to know your oxen teams. Be thankful for them. Watch with steady courage the ones who plough ahead of you and receive, in faith and love, the flame they place into your hands.

2: ELEVEN TEAMS OF OXEN
Suggestions for prayer and reflection

Remembering . . .

During the next few weeks, take a little time in prayer to remember your life, your journey of faith so far, in God's presence.

Re-member-ing means, literally, piecing together again what has become fragmented or broken. Ask God for the grace to *re-member* the fragments of your life in a way that will reveal to you the patterns that are leading towards your wholeness in him.

Try the following exercises:

- Remember the exterior events of your life and your reactions to them. As you remember these events, notice the *gifts* that you have received: skills and talents, gifts of personality, gifts from your circumstances – education, family, friends, jobs, your whole situation in life, gifts of people who have become significant for you.

- Notice how God has been present in your life, and the periods where he appeared to be absent. How has he made himself known to you at special moments? Remember how it felt when he seemed close to you, or far away.

- Notice now how God has been *constantly* present, not just in the special moments. Notice especially how, with hindsight, periods when he felt absent may have prepared you in some way for further growth. Notice how periods of difficulty strengthened you in certain ways, as hard exercise strengthens our muscles. Remember how consolation and new strength has sometimes come when you were 'at the end of the line'. This isn't to pretend to yourself that everything, with hindsight, was 'good'. That would be dishonest and untrue, because we live in a fallen world where evil is endemic. Where honesty prevents you from seeing God in parts of your life, tell him so in your prayer, and express your pain and anger to him freely.

- Become aware of how God touches your unique personality and brings you to life; how he speaks to you through your own personality, your gifts and your decisions. Can you see any concrete examples of how God is using your gifts or working through your decisions now, in your immediate experience?

- Try to describe – or to draw! – your own *images of God*. How does he appear to you – a Father figure, a policeman, a friend, a doctor, a fireman, male or female, distant or close, firm or gentle, judging, guiding or apparently ignoring you? It may be helpful to remember how you thought of God when you were a child and compare those images with the way you see him now. Your childhood images may actually express more honestly what you still, deep down, truly feel. There is no 'right' answer! The purpose of the exercise is to get in touch with the way you are personally relating to God, and how you feel about that relationship.

At every point, express your feelings to God in prayer, without fear, without holding anything back.

Praying with your story

To use Scripture in prayer, read the passage through carefully until you feel 'at home' with it, and ask the Lord to open your heart to discern its personal meanings for you and your own life's journey. This is the basis of all scriptural prayer.

The passages suggested below may help you to explore particular aspects of your own story, with the Lord alongside you. They are only suggestions. Use them only if they are helpful. If you find yourself especially drawn towards a particular passage (either one of these or any other), stay with it. You can be sure that God is wanting to reveal something to you through it. Repeat it as often as you feel drawn to do so. Go back especially to any point where you experienced any kind of strong feeling. These strong feelings (either negative or positive) are signs of deep inner movements in your heart, and may be pointers to where God is acting in your life. These are signals to you that this is an area that should be looked at more closely. Repetition like this can lead to great deepening and healing of a particular aspect of your life. People have been known to spend the whole of an eight-day retreat praying with just one passage that was crucial to their growth.

Genesis 1:26–31: The Creation of Human Life

Reflect on your own beginnings, the 'garden' in which your life has been planted. Notice God's creating energy and joy bringing you to life in so many different ways since you were first conceived.

Notice especially verse 31 and receive its affirmation personally into your heart.

Exodus 2:1-10: The Birth of Moses

Reflect on your early years of growth and change. Let the Lord lead you through any dark experiences of loss, fear, danger or threat. Moses was born into an extremely threatening situation. Are there 'bulrush' times in your experience? Can you trace, with hindsight, the hand of God in the ways you were brought through them?

Where, in the end, was the greater power: in the basket made of reeds, or in the might of the Pharaoh's empire?

Reflect on how God's promise to Moses was brought to fulfilment, and reflect on the promise he has implanted in your own life.

Exodus 13:17-22: The Pillar of Cloud and the Pillar of Fire

Desert times, times of wandering, directionless survival, or even despair. Times when you seem to be going round in circles and getting nowhere? Open up your own desert spaces in prayer and ask the Lord to show you how to recognise your own pillars of cloud and fire in the confusion.

Notice that Moses carries the body of Joseph, the dreamer, across the wilderness to the Promised Land. We too are invited to carry our dreams through our deserts. Notice the dreams that God is asking you to carry, and carry them joyfully.

1 Kings 19:19: The Call of Elisha

You may like to get in touch with your own 'eleven teams of oxen' if this image is helpful.

Reflect in prayer on the events, circumstances and people that have led you further along your path of growth, and helped you plough your furrow. Then see the Lord at their head and feel his spirit running through all your personal line of meaning.

Psalm 139: 'Lord, you have examined me and you know me' (verses 1-16)

Hear the words of the psalm applied to the days of your own life. Reflect on the thoughts expressed in verses 13, 15 and 16, on the infinite value to God of your being, even when you were 'growing in secret in your mother's womb'. Now reflect on the infinite value to God of your inner being, which even now is 'growing in secret' at the heart of your lived life.

Ask the Lord to lead you in prayer to share something of his own deep knowledge of you – that knowledge that all of us long for, yet often seek to avoid.

When you recall the dark and the light times of your own experience, let the words of verse 12 set them into perspective for you.

John 4:5-30: The Woman at the Well

Imagine yourself going to the well to draw the day's water. Encounter Jesus there, a stranger who knows you through and through. Let him engage you in conversation there and let him take you in that conversation wherever he will.

Then return to the village. What difference has the encounter made to your future journeying?

Luke 24:13-35: Walk to Emmaus

Place yourself in imagination alongside the two disciples, in their bewildered disappointment. Allow the stranger to come alongside you. He seems to know nothing about the events of your life, so tell him how it has been for you. Tell him how you are feeling about the course of your life so far, your hopes, your fears, your expectations.

When you reach the crossroads . . . what happens next?

3. SO WHAT WENT WRONG?

We have spent quite some time exploring those elusive questions of 'Who am I?', 'What is the real heart of me all about?', 'What has shaped me into the person I am today?'. I hope that in these explorations you have discovered something of the trace of God's finger in everything that has made you 'you', and everything that is continuing to shape you into 'who you really are'.

Yet we live here in what seems to be a broken world, and our own lives are blighted by an abiding sense of being separated from our source, alienated from our true selves and from each other. Each one of us, today, can look back over what can seem (in the bad times) like a trail of broken dreams and shattered hopes. Or perhaps our hidden Godseed appears to have amounted to nothing more exciting than a middle-aged couch potato.

So what went wrong? Can we simply be satisfied by the conventional religious language of 'sin' and somehow make it fit that inner howling that comes from the deep awareness of something badly wrong, that no amount of theology is going to cure for us?

In the first stage of the *Spiritual Exercises*, Ignatius invites the pilgrim to reflect on what we might call *the scale of the problem*. What does 'fallenness' really mean, in our lived experience, and can it be that God loves us unconditionally, through it and beyond it all? Or is that just wishful thinking?

To know the reality of our brokenness and our separation from God, in our gut and not just in our heads, is a harrowing experience. We enter into this experience only when we know, in the same deep-felt way, God's unconditional love for us, which holds our brokenness in gently sheltering hands, like a wounded bird.

Discovering the Godseed in our hearts, noticing the golden threads of

God's unconditional love holds our brokenness in gently sheltering hands

meaning in our own life's journey, and becoming increasingly aware of God's continuing presence in our lives and in everything and everyone we encounter, are just a few of the possibilities for opening ourselves up more and more to this unconditional love, even as we stand face-to-face with the nature and extent of our own fallenness and the fallenness of all creation.

A couple of parables from my own life's journey have helped me to make this connection between God's free-flowing love for us, and our own imprisonment in our brokenness and the world's . . .

Lock 46

Many years ago I worked in a place not far from the Trent and Mersey canal. During lunchbreaks I would often wander through the surrounding fields, down to the towpath, and walk along the canal for a while. In those days there was a good deal less pressure at work, and extended lunch-hours were a luxury we tended to take for granted.

All kinds of unpleasantness have intervened between those happy memories, and the place where I find myself today, including the loss of that job, and the relative security it once held for me. Some of that unpleasantness was undoubtedly of my own making. Some of it seems to be endemic in the way life hurts everyone in some way or other, as the years go on.

As chance (or God?) would have it, however, I found myself back there recently, sent by my present employer, an agency, to carry out a short-term contract in the place where I had once been a 'permanent' employee. One lunchtime, when the sun was shining, I decided that I would risk a half-hour absence from my 'contractor's desk', because I suddenly had the urge to go back through the fields of my memory and seek out the canal towpath again. The walk, stolen out of the middle of a harassed day, became a prayer, and gave me a perspective on my own life's journey that permanently changed my way of seeing things.

It was a lovely warm, mellow October day. The clouds were scudding across a pale blue sky and the leaves collected in floating brown islands by the lock gates. Lock 46, as the sign read, became my place of rest for a space, a million miles away from the unreal realities of the office. It was a dappled day and the sunlight warmed my heart into responsiveness, like a lover's touch. 'My peace I give you', the unspoken words reverberated, 'not as the world gives.'

From time to time a canal narrow boat passed through the lock. It amazed me how this gently flowing water, so peaceful in the autumn sunshine, suddenly took on the power to raise several tons of iron and steel by all those feet between where I was sitting and the deep drop to the lock floor. And I knew, as I watched, that God is doing the same for me. His Spirit flows so gently and unobtrusively through the landscape of my heart, but when its power is called for, it can raise me from the depths of my unfreedom to the heights of his love, and free me to continue my journey, borne on this fragile flow that seems so ephemeral, yet runs eternally.

I let the breeze caress me, and it told me the same kind of truth. It's only the breeze that reminds me that there is air all around me at all. I only notice its presence when it is stirred by storm and currents. There was just a gentle breeze that day, just enough to flick the clouds into playfulness and rustle the dying leaves. Yet it carried the seeds of next year's springtime, and its every molecule surrounded me with the oxygen I need to stay alive. What unseen powers are these, in wind and water, all sunshine-dappled and charged with an energy that is capable of setting a universe in motion, but also with a love that is able – and desiring – to touch *my* heart into peace?

But I had extended my lunchbreak too far already. I made my way back, past a contemplative fisherman, who was surely reaching for his own peace too. Past the notice on the canal-side by the pub, which read: '*48-hour moorings only.*' This week had put that notice up in *my* life too. Here I was, just a contractor back here in the place where I had worked for so many years. A different desk each day, wherever there happened to be space. And a borrowed lap-top computer, plugged in wherever I could find a vacant socket. I hardly knew anyone here now, and hardly anyone knew me. The foxes have holes and the birds of the air have nests, but a contract worker has nowhere to plug in her laptop, at least not for more than a 48-hour mooring!

It all reflected my deep sense of inner homelessness, but today it didn't disturb me. In fact it stirred some deep desire to be with the water and the air in the life-bringing, power-in-gentleness of their flow, and with the sunlight that filtered through the yellowing leaves to warm me into joy. I can't catch the water or hold the breeze or store up the sunlight, any more than I can be sure where my workplace will be tomorrow. But this graced hour, in the 48-hour mooring, seemed more real to me than all the structures I had thought were my life's harbour. There was peace in the flow. Not the peace I might have sought, in the strength of my own foolish wisdom, but the peace that God had set out before me in the wise folly of the falling leaves that settle for a moment on the water that flows through Lock 46, and then are gone.

All this had been a lived, *and felt*, experience of God's unconditional love.

But perhaps the most far-reaching grace of this lunchtime retreat to Lock 46 came when I realised that I myself feel rather like a narrow boat in the lock chamber with the lock gates firmly closed on me. Because I have no real knowledge of what came before the lock chamber, if anything, or what will follow after, the lock chamber itself seems to be all there is. I believe, in faith, that there is a canal that has brought me here and that will, in some mysterious way, take me further, but in my *lived experience* it usually doesn't feel like that. It often feels as though I am here in a deep, dark prison, facing brick walls on every side, and with no way out that my mind can guess at or imagine. A pointless and a daunting place to be. If I think about my condition at all, I start to examine every brick or stone in that lock chamber, as if it were the whole arena of my living, and in the hope that a minute examination of its walls might reveal some meaning in it, or some way of dealing with it.

This process, of examining my prison walls, though it may be absorbing, is ultimately rather futile, because it completely lacks *perspective*. The lock chamber makes no sense at all unless you know about the canal. Without the canal the boat is, truly, just a prisoner in a pointless place. But when the reality of the canal is felt, and embraced, *then* the transformation happens. Then the lock chamber is seen to be the place, and the *only* place, where God's grace might be inflowing, to raise me to the place where I must be, if my homeward journey with him is to go on into what is still unexplored.

To raise me? Or to lower me? Sometimes, as I look back, I can see that grace has flowed into my empty lock and lifted me up, on its tide, into God's presence, with no effort of my own. But sometimes it seemed to do just the opposite. Grace seemed to be draining away, and I felt myself sinking lower and lower between the dark, damp stones, to be left alone in the very darkest depths of myself, until God opened the lock gates and set me free to journey on. Downstream, or upstream? Either way transforms the dark imprisonment of the lock chamber of our life into the very place which is making possible the onward movement on a journey that is infinitely larger and greater than our caged hearts can understand.

My fallenness, it seems to me, has something to do with this loss of perspective. It is about my feeling of the radical separation of myself from the flow of life and of love and of God that alone makes sense of me. But the flow of love and of God never ceases to be there for me, and even as I sit captive in my lock chamber, not knowing where I am or why, God is already manning the lock gates and bringing me, in his own time and his own way, to the point of readiness for moving on.

A pointless place to be~
or the only gateway to the
onward journey?

The signpost city

Perhaps we only begin to understand the nature of our imprisonment
when we have at least *begun* to be freed from it ...

I lived for several years in Berlin, during the time of the Cold War. Our
flat was in a run-down inner city area in the north of the town, less than
fifty metres from the Wall. We were often awakened at night by the sound
of shots and the flash of flares. During this period we also experienced a
blockade preventing the normal flow of traffic along any of the three land
routes between West Berlin and West Germany. The only way for us, in
those years, to travel beyond the city limits, was to use one of the three air
corridors to the West. Apart from that, Berlin, at that time, could be encap-
sulated in the Underground map. A network of streets and squares and
junctions named after unknown and, for me, unimaginable, places in the
lost hinterland of East Germany.

It never occurred to me that these were anything more than names on a street plan. I walked the avenues and shopped in the squares. I travelled to work along the network. I could get onto the Underground anywhere in West Berlin and within half an hour I would hear the words: '*Endstation. Alle aussteigen.*' 'This is the end of the line. Please leave the train.'

And it was so. Beyond the terminus was no-man's land with its watch-towers, and mines, its Wall and its barbed wire, and its Full Stop.

This memory of Berlin returned to me very vividly one day in prayer. Suddenly I could see myself like the beleaguered city. That was exactly how I felt, when I started to realise my separateness from God. A little space, a little bit of consciousness and choice, a little tangle of loving and fearing, longing and hiding, desiring and rejecting, but totally cut off from my hinterland. Like a besieged city I am surrounded by unscaleable walls and hostile guards, and I am occupied by enemy forces. Only the air corridors of my prayer open up a slender connection to my eternal reality. Even my food and drink have to be air-lifted to me, and if those supplies fail, I die.

Then my prayer led me on into the city itself. With these just-awakening eyes I began to see what was happening there. The city that I myself had seen to be an imprisoned, disconnected island, dependent for every morsel of food and every means of living, upon supplies from outside, and besieged by all the machinery of war and oppression – the city teeming with its trapped and captive inhabitants who can't go an inch beyond the limits of their tether – that same city thinks it is the bastion of freedom! And my city, my inner city, that depends on God just to stay in existence, my city too thinks it is both independent and free! Not only that, it thinks it is some sort of model and defender of other people's freedom. Just as West Berlin set itself up (with American persuasion) as the 'shop window of the West', so I can all too easily start to regard my inner city as if it were something for others to emulate.

The prayer humbled and mortified me, and left me at God's feet in shame. For the first time I could see the total absurdity and the arrogance of my condition and, perhaps, of the whole human condition.

At first I could feel only the despair of the situation, and my absolute helplessness in it. I felt my own disconnectedness from God. I felt it deeply, and horribly. My world, I realised, was built on quicksand, and it could col-lapse at any moment. Just as a Soviet blockade could have cut me off from bread and water, so the blockade of sin cuts me off from God . . . and I die. The logic is relentless, and we are all in it together – helpless together and condemned together . . . unless . . .

In 1989, a miracle happened, that nobody had really dared to hope for. The Berlin Wall came down. The whole country was opened up again, and it was possible, for the first time in over forty years, actually to go to the places that these so-familiar street names had pointed to. I shall never forget the discovery that the street names and Underground stations I had known actually related to real places in the surrounding regions.

It was only as we drove through the towns and villages of Brandenburg and Mecklenburg that the Underground map, my experience of Berlin, so completely circumscribed by circumstance, began to unfold, as a butterfly emerges from its awakening and tentatively spreads its damp wings. Every town and village connected to, and gave its name to, one of those familiar streets or squares or junctions. The end of the line wasn't a no-man's land or an impassable barrier, but a real place, with houses, trees, cows and concrete, dustbins and maypoles, and all the sweat and tenderness of a living community. One after another my underground stations came to life in these towns and villages of eastern Germany. The hinterland was no longer a shadowy, impenetrable mystery, surrounding the vortex of lived life in the amputated city of Berlin. No. Things had turned inside out. The hinterland was the reality, to which the enclosed, imprisoned city had been but the signpost.

It made me think differently about life and death. What if that shadowy mystery beyond the span of our years turns out to be the real country, to which our earthly days are just the fragmented signposts? What if the unconscious realms in which our conscious minds are floating turn out to be the embryonic sac that is beckoning us towards a Reality far beyond imagination? What if that of my life that seems so total, so final and so absolute turns out to be just the first tentative beginning, and suppose my prayer were to be the map into the hinterland of my eternal reality?

And how reluctant we are to let go of the containing walls and to risk a life beyond the circumscription. Easier, surely, to survive in the slavery of Egypt than to venture into Sinai, to convince ourselves that our slavery is freedom and that our helplessness is a proud independence.

The map changes radically when our walls come down and the real roads, that were always there, though impassable, are opened up. Then the hinterland becomes the heartland, where real life can really be lived.

My fallenness, I begin to understand, has a great deal to do with my determination to attend to the signposts and to mistake them for the reality of things – to become so attached to my wrong perceptions of what is 'real', that I have become blinded to the fullness of reality, to the extent that, if you show me a caterpillar, I will adamantly resist, and even ridicule, any suggestion that it contains a hidden butterfly. In my fallenness, I am equally blind to the possibility of my own embryonic butterfly and – even more seriously – I am blind to the butterfly in *you*.

Sin, perhaps, is like holding a daffodil bulb in our hands but neglecting to plant it in our life's soil because we refuse to believe that it contains a flower. Yet alongside all of all our flat refusals to believe, the gardener plants us, nonetheless, and tends us lovingly, because he knows who we are, and holds everything we shall become, in his gentle hands.

A baby in the minefield

Whatever is going to be necessary to redeem this fallenness, I realise, slowly and painfully, is going to turn my own certainties and expectations upside down and inside out. The days of prayer that had taken me to Lock 46 and then back to Berlin, now took me to the foot of the cross, where a man born to be king hung, mangled and broken. He had come into the lost city, breaching its defences from outside, and willingly joined himself to its despair and perdition. He had come to lead me out, hopeless and bedraggled and mortally wounded, and carry me back home. He hung there because he had engaged the occupying forces on my behalf, and had conquered . . .

But it didn't look like victory, from where I was standing. It looked quite the opposite. Why was he hanging there? Why did his victory look like defeat? How did he break through the fortifications?

The answer came to me in the shape of a tiny Baby, the seed from which a Kingdom would spring. Just a shoot on a dead branch. So small that it wouldn't activate the mines all around me, and so insignificant that the guards wouldn't notice its slipping beneath the barbed wire. So helpless that it was hardly worth bothering to kill. 'Seek for the same helpless insignificance in yourself', the Child seemed to say. 'Let that be your key to freedom.'

To take this total reversal of my flawed human logic on board was going to require a revolution ...

But revolution is a real possibility, and miracles can be prayed for and expected ...

3: SO WHAT WENT WRONG?
Suggestions for prayer and reflection

> *Yahweh says this:*
> *'A curse on the man who puts his trust in man,*
> *who relies on things of flesh,*
> *whose heart turns from Yahweh.*
> *He is like dry scrub in the wastelands:*
> *if good comes, he has no eyes for it,*
> *he settles in the parched places of the wilderness,*
> *a salt land, uninhabited.*
> *A blessing on the man who puts his trust in Yahweh,*
> *with Yahweh for his hope.*
> *He is like a tree by the waterside*
> *that thrusts its roots to the stream:*
> *when the heat comes it feels no alarm,*
> *its foliage stays green;*
> *it has no worries in a year of drought,*
> *and never ceases to bear fruit.'*

(Jeremiah 17:5-8)

Read these words, slowly and peacefully, and re-read them again and again for as long as you feel drawn to stay with them. In your imagination, picture the two trees that Jeremiah speaks of: the 'dry scrub in the waste-lands' and the 'tree by the waterside that thrusts its roots to the stream'.

Let yourself enter, imaginatively, into the life of the first tree, the 'dry scrub'. Try to feel its thirst, its brittleness, its sense of being disconnected from the source of its being. Feel the burning heat of the desert. Taste the corrosive saltiness of the dry air. Feel the stinging in your eyes, blinding you to the world around you. Imagine the gradual dying away of all your life energy, until you sink into the sand and are forgotten.

Now try to enter into the life of the second tree, which grows at the waterside. Feel your roots going deep into the cool earth, and finding the life-sustaining water. Notice the cover of green foliage, shielding you from the burning sun. Enjoy the taste of the fruit growing on your boughs. Relax in the certainty that no drought can destroy you because your roots are connected to the ground water.

Bring your feelings about the two trees to God in your prayer, perhaps expressing your distress at those aspects of your being that are disconnected from him, and your joy at those things in you that are rooted in your trust of him.

❊

Look back over the events of the last twenty-four hours. Notice just one special moment, or event, or encounter that has given you joy and helped you to remember that you are loved. Look back over your life's journey, remembering those milestones that seem, with hindsight, truly to have made your life worthwhile. Remember one special person who has made you aware of God's unconditional love for you, perhaps by giving you their own. Offer God your gratitude for these repeated signs of his love for you, and ask him for the grace to trust in that love when you are feeling hurt and broken.

❊

Imagine yourself as a wounded bird savaged by a cat, or as an animal caught in a trap, or as a small child who has hurt herself because she disobeyed her parents' instructions. Now, without offering any excuses or justifications or reproaches against what has harmed you, just let yourself be gathered up by God and held gently in the palm of his hand. Be still, and simply *know* that he is God, who loves you and desires your wholeness so much that he is ready to die for it.

❊

Is there a situation in your life that feels like the 'lock chamber', where you feel trapped, and where all your efforts and desires seem quite meaningless, and there seems to be no way out? You might like to lay this situation before God in your prayer, and ask him to show you any ways in which it has meaning and significance beyond the results (or lack of them) that you are able to see. For example, you may spend all your days in a job that seems to benefit no-one and makes you frustrated. Let your job unfold in your prayer, and ask God to change your perspective, to see any ways in which it makes a difference whether you do your work with joy or with resistance. If you feel able to do so, try to make a real human contact with a work colleague or another person who is trapped in a similar situation, and listen to their feelings about where they find themselves. If you can do this, then, however pointless your work may seem, it will have become the place where true human communion has become possible.

✿

God is in all things and therefore God is in the 'lock chamber'. Try placing some symbol of your faith in the place where you feel 'trapped', for example, in the office, in the kitchen, in the car. This could be a candle, or a flower, an icon or some small thing that is significant only to yourself. Let this become a constant reminder to you that this place of your apparent imprisonment is sacred space, because God is there. Similarly, try taking five minutes every so often during the day to be away from your work, perhaps just by taking a short walk in the garden or down the corridor or round the car park, or even to the coffee machine and back. Be deliberate about taking this time just for yourself alone, but, equally deliberately, ask God to walk with you. Don't try to make it a time of elaborate 'prayer'. Just let it be time when you remember, consciously, that you and God are in this thing together. In this way your five minutes will be sacred, and the whole day will be touched by this sacred time, as the Sabbath touches the whole week into sacredness.

✿

Can you name any of the 'signposts' that have pointed you towards God as your life has unfolded? Now, in the honesty of your own heart, do you notice any points when you have stayed with the 'signposts' instead of walking on beyond them? For example, you may have become fixed on a particular kind of liturgy, and feel 'bereft' if you can't find a church which is 'on your wavelength', or you may be becoming trapped in a compulsive need to pray in a particular way, at a particular time or in a special place, and feel disturbed if anything interferes with this. If you find any 'long-term settlements' like this, just ask God to help you see beyond them, to where he is beckoning you forward. But be gentle with yourself.

※

The gospel, on which we have chosen to found our lives, is about the power of God coming to us in the helplessness of a refugee baby and of a condemned and executed man. Are there any events or turning points in your own life where you know that God's power was active in you at a time when you yourself felt most helpless or inadequate? Recall, in prayer, one of these times and try to take into your heart the fact that 'God's power is seen most surely in our weakness'.

※

We have almost all been brought up to value our 'independence'. What aspects of your independence do you especially cherish? Now make a list of all the things that your 'independence' depends on – a car, for example, or the maintenance of your good health, the availability of a child-minder, a reliable cattery to look after your pet while you are on retreat, un-interrupted gas and water supplies, an understanding doctor, a job that doesn't require you to work on Sundays, a word processor that corrects your spelling, a fridge that saves you from having to go to the shops every day, a wife who remembers where you left your glasses?

These are just a few examples of the very many things we take for granted in our assumptions about independence. I remember especially the day I dropped my driving glasses on the doorstep, and realised how the most trivial accident like this was able to immobilise me and to rob me of my much cherished 'vision'! It also made me realise how heavily I depend on my 'emergency services', like a willing and competent optician, and on the money needed to pay for them in my hour of need.

4. THE COPERNICAN REVOLUTION

Transformation is going to involve a revolution! In this chapter we look at what happens when we make the earth-shattering discovery, like Copernicus before us, that the sun does not revolve around the earth, but the earth revolves around the sun, or, in more personal language, neither God nor his creation revolve around *us*, but we and all creation revolve around, and are centred in, God.

At this point in our growth-path towards our deepest and eternal reality, we have to make a radical switch of focus. God challenges us to cease to be 'self'-centred, that is, in orbit around our own kingdoms, and to become '*God-centred*'. This is an uncomfortable moment. More probably, for most of us, it is an ongoing discomfort that never goes away throughout our adult lives. Once we have become aware of the way things really *are* organised, we can never again be quite comfortable with ourselves, when we are living as though things were still the way our illusions had seduced us into believing.

We can see the effect of facing the sun, the God-centre, or facing the centre of our own kingdoms, in the example shown in the picture on the next page. What happens when we are orientated towards our own kingdoms, and away from the 'sun' – our God-centre? Where does the shadow fall? How does it leave us feeling? What do we have to do to change things? In fact all we need to do is to turn round. There is no requirement to walk all the way back, retracing the wrong pathways in reverse. As soon as we make the radical shift of *focus*, we automatically expose ourselves to the sun's rays. What does that do to the shadow?

On a smaller scale, I remember, as a child, being mystified when my parents used to complain, as I sat reading or doing my homework, with my back to the window or to the lamp, that I was 'sitting in my own light'. At the time I thought it was just another way the grown-ups had devised to

I am directed away from God.

I am turned away from the Light of my truest centre.

I am in desolation.

Shadow, darkness, fear

I am directed towards God.

I am facing the Light of my own truest centre.

I am in consolation.

the darkness is behind me.

interfere with my freedom and find fault with my way of doing things, and I often stubbornly refused to turn round and enjoy the full stream of light on my work. Of course, if I did do the sensible thing, it made a big difference to my ability to discern things . . . reluctant though I might have been to admit it!

Now, on reflection, the words 'sitting in my own light' leap off the paper and hit me between the eyes. What a description of fallenness! Here we sit, basking in our own light (rather than in God's), so sure of its continuance and its glory, while all the time we are actually casting our own shadow over everything and everyone in our line of vision.

There are two major problems with this position . . .

The first is that, like the earth, we don't have such a thing as 'our own light'. That's not how things are. The light that may seem to illumine us is not ours at all, but the reflected light of the sun, and, ultimately, of God. This is a fundamental difference between the Creator and the creature. Recognising our 'creaturehood' is probably the most painful part of the

Copernican revolution. It means letting go of that certainty that we are somehow the source, or at least the controller, of our own being.

The second problem is the matter of the shadow. If I remain with my back to the light source, or, rather, to God who is the source of my being, my own bulk (which is just an image for my 'ego') will overshadow all that I do – all my efforts, all my relationships, all my journey. Not only will I not be able to see the way ahead, because of my own shadow, but I will cast the darkness over others. I will make the world a darker place. And, of course, the bigger my ego, the larger and darker will be the shadow I cast.

There is another subtle twist when it comes to deluding ourselves that we are suns, rather than planets. Having convinced ourselves that we are 'our own light' and our own centre of gravity, the next step is not far behind, when we begin to think that other beings should revolve around us. In this way we can set up whole systems or hierarchies of 'fallenness', and the shadow of sin looms ever larger and more darkly over life on earth. We, who were created, as Ignatius says, 'to praise, reverence and serve God', begin to spend our energies in trying to arrange that others, and indeed that all of creation, should exist to praise, reverence and serve *us*.

When we look at things in this light, we begin to see that 'sin' is not just a shopping-list of misdemeanours to bring to the confessional. It is a radical inside-out-ness, and the more we try to sort it out for ourselves, the more entangled we will become.

To see this dynamic in action, it's usually easier to watch it happening *to* us, rather than *because of* us. Perhaps you are aware of situations or relationships where you feel that, though you are not centred on God, you are not entirely centred on yourself either. It may well be, then, that you are being drawn into orbit around someone else's (false) centre, and their magnetic field, so to speak. This may be through your own choice, or through their manipulative influence (deliberate or unconscious) upon you. Either way, it is not helping you to draw closer to God: rather, it is impeding your journey and undermining your inner freedom, and may need to be prayerfully examined and resisted.

If we recognise God as our 'sun', that is, the source and upholder of all our being, and ourselves as 'planets' whose natural movement is to be in orbit around our Source, then we can come closer to the real meaning of two words that are used by masters of the spiritual life, including Ignatius: the words 'consolation' and 'desolation' – words which carry rather a different meaning in the context of our inner journey than the meanings we associate with them in everyday speech.

What do we mean when we talk of 'consolation' and 'desolation'? We are really only talking about the state of being 'with the sun' or 'out of the sun', and the bottom line is this: which direction is our life taking – towards God, or away from him? Turning, or *metanoia*, can sound like a sudden, dramatic conversion exercise, and for some people it may come as a one-off Damascus experience. But for most it is a gradual process that extends through life. And even for the Damascus people, the choice continues in every lived moment, in every choice we make, however apparently trivial. Every minute of our lives is a moment in which we can be 'towards the sun' or 'away from it'; we can be moving towards consolation or drifting into desolation.

How do we tell the difference? And what can we do about it? Before we go on to reflect more deeply (in later chapters) on the movements of our moods, we need first to get in touch with Ignatius' understanding of how our moods will reflect a different underlying pattern depending on whether the *general* direction of our lives is towards God or away from him. To allay any dismay at this point, it is important to stress that anyone who is reading a book like this, and is seeking to deepen their prayer is certainly *not*, in a general way, moving away from God. We may, however, all too easily, find ourselves *temporarily* drifting away from our desired destination, and many of us will recall times in our lives when this state of things was more lasting and ingrained.

Ignatius explains the underlying patterns of the moods of the two orientations (towards, or away from, God) like this:

- For those drifting *away* from God, the action of God in their lives disturbs them and churns up their moods, creating peacelessness, while the things that come from their own kingdoms make them feel good and leave them apparently contented.
- For those whose lives are moving *towards* God, the opposite effects are apparent: when God is touching them, they feel at peace and they know that somehow they are on solid ground; when they are (hopefully temporarily) attending to their own kingdoms, they feel that they are not really 'living true', and they experience inner turmoil.

Another way of looking at the effects of our inner movements is through the example of the tide ebbing and flowing onto a beach, as the picture shows.

My underlying heart-movement is like a flow-tide, focused on God and drawn towards him.

My underlying heart-movement is like an ebb-tide, drifting away from God.

If we imagine that the beach represents our true centre and home in God, and the destination of our journeying, we can see that the sea is either moving *towards* the beach (flow-tide) or *away from* it (ebb-tide). In the same way, our hearts, or our truest centres, are directed either towards, or away from, God. This represents the general orientation of our lives. Now look at the effect of the winds, which we might compare to the action of what Ignatius calls 'the spirits'. Imagine the effect on a swimmer who is moving, in general terms, with the tidal flow, when the wind is blowing *against* the direction of the tide: if the wind is blowing out to sea, then it will impede the progress of the person swimming with the flow-tide by working in the opposite direction; if the wind is blowing in from offshore, it will accelerate the swimmer's progress. The opposite effects can be seen in the way these same winds work on a swimmer who is moving out to sea on an ebb-tide.

If we translate this into the language of our spiritual journey, we can see that when we are directed towards our home in God, a wind in the opposite direction will cause turbulence and act obstructively. Yet the same wind would be perceived as a benefit to those whose journey is directed away from God. If we now acknowledge that these winds represent the creative and destructive spirits, or movements, working in our hearts, we can begin to understand how a spirit, or an inner movement that speeds and affirms the journey of a pilgrim on his way towards God would appear as a movement of *opposition* for a person whose life is directed away from God.

Since we can assume that all of us who are joined together in the fellowship of this book, to deepen our life in God, have the same basic orientation towards God, and towards our home in him (the 'beach'), we can see from this example that the 'bad spirits' are like the wind blowing against us and making us feel that we are up against blocks and obstructions, and experiencing turbulence and distress, while the 'good spirits' are like the wind blowing from behind us, giving us a sense of support, encouragement and apparently speeding our journey and cooperating with it.

Of course these are only metaphors. Not everyone today would readily identify with Ignatius' notion of the 'spirits' as separate, objectively real entities, sent either to try us or to cheer us. Yet all of us know that we experience these different movements in our hearts. Sometimes they clearly spring from our own inner lives, our moods and our intentions. Sometimes they appear to beset us from outside, for no apparent reason, and very occasionally we may experience a real sense of being at the mercy of evil forces beyond our human comprehension. Our aim here is not to try to identify the various ways in which negative or positive inner movements arise, but rather to understand their *effects*, so that we can become better able to respond to them. We do this by welcoming and giving thanks for the times of consolation, when the winds are 'with us', and by being on guard when we encounter the movements of desolation when the winds are 'against us'.

A crisis in the tunnel?

Ignatius gives us an absolute rule for handling desolation:

> *When in desolation, don't take life-changing decisions, and don't go back on a decision that you took during a period of consolation.*

If you translate this into the language of the tides and the winds, it would be equivalent to sensing an opposing wind when you are swimming to shore on a flow-tide, and, because you meet the opposition of the wind and experience the turbulence, you decide to turn round and let the wind blow you back out to sea. How many of us have had such an experience, when circumstances turned against us and our response was something like: 'I always knew it was pointless; I don't know what possessed me to try. I'm quitting.'

A friend of mine, who has given permission for her story to be shared, recently suffered a tragic bereavement, which left her shocked and stunned for many months. A few months after this loss, she and her husband had a holiday together on a canal narrow boat, and afterwards she shared her thoughts on how it felt to be travelling through a tunnel. To enter the tunnel, she said, was like entering 'a dark night', such as the one she had just experienced in the loss of her friend. Even the slightest bends in the length of the tunnel mean that the light, from the exit, is obscured. In a tunnel you can lose all sense of perspective; you can almost forget that there was ever daylight. This is how she describes it:

> You cannot see even your hand in front of you without a light to guide you. The exit is not visible as you go through the tunnel; you have to trust that it is there, once you have entered the tunnel's mouth. It is an unpleasant experience, because of the difficulties encountered along the way – narrowly missing other boats, scraping or bumping into the walls, the smells, the dark, the diesel fumes that hang in the air and choke you . . .

This is a vivid picture of how spiritual 'desolation' can feel, though of course each person's experience is unique. Small wonder, that in such inner circumstances, we are tempted to give up, turn back, change direction and reverse the decision we first made to make the journey that has led us into this tunnel. It was at this point in her reflection that my friend made her own discovery of Ignatius' wisdom:

> You can't turn a forty-foot boat round in a tunnel, so once you have started you have to continue. To reverse is to lose your steering control.

This picture is one of the most vivid images I have ever encountered of the reality of Ignatius' warning about not changing course during a period of desolation. It bears prayerful reflection:

- If you try to turn a forty-foot boat round in a tunnel, you will cause a thoroughgoing shipwreck. Your life, and your journey with God are on board that boat. Don't risk sinking them forever in the depths of that dark tunnel.
- Nor is backpedalling a realistic alternative: it doesn't work, because it robs you of your steering control. Difficult enough to reverse safely in a car, but try walking backwards in a straight line with your eyes closed for any distance. At best you may get back to where you began, albeit with bumps and scars and gashes from your blind collisions on the reverse journey. But is that really where you want to be – back where you began?

And so, my friend realised, out of her own deeply felt 'dark night' experience, that the tunnel was indeed the only way to move onwards, towards the desired destination, and that all tunnels, however dark, do come to an end. The reality of the journey is not the tunnel but the canal, not the period of dark desolation, but the reality of God's light forever shining, even when we do not see it. She concludes her story:

> When you emerge on the other side, the light seems brighter, the birdsong sweeter and the dappling in the water more beautiful. You see the world with new eyes because of the darkness behind you. You have arrived at a new place further on in your journey.

No turning in the tunnel ---

In the next chapter we will look more deeply into the question of how to recognise our moods of consolation and desolation and where their roots might be located.

Meanwhile, we might reflect on the question: *'Whose kingdom am I really serving: my own or God's?'* And while we might be able to answer that question positively, acknowledging God's kingship, in a *general* way, how does it look when we reflect honestly over the *particular* details of, say, the past twenty-four hours? A deeper look at our changing moods and reactions may tell another story.

4: THE COPERNICAN REVOLUTION
Suggestions for prayer and reflection

> 'May Yahweh bless you and keep you:
> may Yahweh let his face shine upon you and be gracious to you;
> may Yahweh uncover his face to you,
> and bring you peace.'
>
> (Numbers 6:24-6)

Read this text slowly and prayerfully, letting its meanings and its resonances soak deeply into your heart. Read it over and over, as a cow chews its cud, slowly extracting its special flavour and absorbing its nourishment into your WHO-centre, to feed the roots of the WHO you are becoming.

If any phrase or word attracts you especially, stay with it and repeat it to yourself, savouring it and letting God be in it for you.

Allow yourself simply to *be*, in stillness of heart and mind, before God whose face is shining upon you, warming you into eternal life. Be present to him, as he is to you, simply absorbing his love and his grace. Relax into his depths and let him open up your own depths to the coming of his springtime.

※

Has there been a time in your life when you were consistently drifting away from God, either by accident or deliberately? Recall that time now in prayer and offer it to God for his healing and forgiveness.

Remember the circumstances in which you changed direction, maybe suddenly, maybe gradually. Remember where you were living, what you were doing, how old you were at the time. Recall any other human companions who played a part in helping you to turn back to God. Remember and express your gratitude to God.

※

Look back over the past twenty-four hours. Did you experience any 'contra winds' during that time? Any 'following winds'? How did they make you feel?

Can you recall a time when you have made a decision to do something when you were in 'consolation', but then reversed that decision when the winds started to blow against you? Can you recall a time when you have stayed with a decision made in consolation, even though you came up against the 'contra winds' of desolation and turmoil? Compare your feelings now about those two situations.

爨

Reflect on the question: *'Whose kingdom am I really serving?':* My own kingdom? Another person's kingdom? God's kingdom?' Apply it to the specific events of the past day, or week.

To decide whose kingdom is being served by a particular course of action, it is helpful to open up the real motives for what is being done, and to do this with complete honesty before God in prayer. As an example, we might hear a politician declaring that he is taking a controversial course of action because it is 'in the national interest', but if we look more deeply we can see that the main motivator is the forthcoming election, or the need to save face at tomorrow's cabinet meeting.

Warning: It is very easy to answer the question for other people's actions and decisions! It is far from easy to exercise the same degree of honesty in ourselves! To do so, we need God, and prayer and humility (and a sense of humour!).

5. THE NETTLE-BED AND THE ROSE-GARDEN

Tracking our moods

We all know that we are subject to moods which appear to change unpredictably and often uncontrollably. In the last chapter we noticed that there is a fundamental difference between the feelings we sometimes experience of 'being on solid ground', or of 'living true', and the opposite feelings of being 'at odds with ourselves' and in a state of inner turmoil. In this chapter we will try to discover the underlying patterns of these moods and what they can show us of our journey with God.

As we noticed in the last chapter, it is taken as a fact of our lives that our *basic* orientation is towards God, otherwise we would not be seeking to deepen our lives in him in this way. It follows, then, that when we experience the 'solid' feelings, these are springing, however remotely, from God's action upon us. When we experience feelings of turmoil, these will have their ultimate source in something that is not of God, but has to do with our own kingdoms.

Tracing the moods of the day

To get in touch with the changing moods of your lived experience, try this exercise: first steady and still yourself, until you feel that you are in your 'WHO' centre. Now look back, over the last twenty-four hours, or possibly over a longer period, perhaps a week, or even a year. Simply replay the time under review prayerfully, and allow the dominant moods of that period to surface again. It may be helpful to make a note (at least mentally, perhaps written down) of what points in the review period you touched on 'solid' feelings and when you touched on 'turmoil'. Undoubtedly both kinds of feelings will have been present, to some degree, in any period of time, and there is no reason to feel guilty about the latter.

The next stage is to allow God, in the prayer, to lead us down to the real roots of those feelings and those moods. If I felt a surge of rage about something, or a wave of fear or apprehension, what prompted it? Someone trod on one of my cherished dreams, perhaps, or offended my pride, or bumped into some 'furniture' in my secret inner room. If that happened, where exactly was the sore spot located, and does it remind me of other times when the same sore spot has been touched on? What is that sore spot really about? Can we put a name to it, and 'own' it? Have a look at the picture of the nettle-bed and see whether any personal connections come to mind.

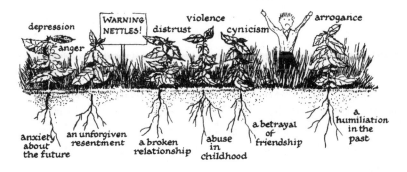

Now let's look at those moments when we were on solid ground. What was the trigger for those feelings? What was I doing at the time? Who was I with? What was said or done to kindle the good feeling? Perhaps it was a moment in touch with God's creation, and I felt my own deep connection to it. Perhaps it was a moment of insight, when I felt that God had given me a flash of understanding about myself, or a situation or a relationship. Perhaps I was touched unexpectedly by the kindness and love of another, or my own feelings of love and compassion were triggered by the needs of someone else. Where was that point of stillness and of peace located? Does it remind me of other similar moments in my experience? Where is its real source, and what new growth does it lead to? Just as with the sore spots, we can name it and own it. It is ours – a gift from God. The rose-garden picture on the next page may help to kindle your personal positive recollections.

The exercise just described is commonly called a *Review of Consciousness* prayer. Ignatius urged his companions to make a review of consciousness prayer every day, even if they had no time for any other form of prayer. In this way he taught them how to track their own moods and discover the deeper movements in their hearts, learning to recognise the 'solid ground' moods as *'consolation'*, and the moods of inner turmoil as *'desolation'*. Over time this practice will help us to see where the deepest desires of our hearts really lie, and it will reveal where our deepest unease is located. It will also help us to distinguish between the movements of God within us, which result in consolation, and the movements that spring from our own kingdoms or from the pressure of other people's kingdoms, and which tend towards desolation.

Noticing our inner furniture

The 'furniture' in our 'inner rooms' is particularly accident-prone, and it has the major disadvantage of being invisible to those unfortunates who may well crash into it without warning, and of being invisible to ourselves as well, unless and until we let God reveal it to us in our prayer and our reflection on what is going on in our lives. We all have this kind of 'furniture', which may be to do with bad memories and experiences or some irrational prejudice that has its roots in our own histories. The picture overleaf shows an example.

The person on the left is happy to show off her new baby, but her friend on the right is suddenly brought up against the raw memories of a lost, or perhaps aborted, child, memories she thought she had dealt with, but which are actually waiting to surface at the slightest opportunity. The joy of the one person and the grief of the other are on a collision course, and neither may understand the reasons for the tension that is brewing between them.

The trick with the inner furniture is not to try to get rid of it – no one

On a collision course...

...with her
inner
furniture...

can do that; we are all populated by our memories and our fears – but to make it *visible* to ourselves. Once we know that it is there, and what it looks like, people will still bump into it, but we will have moved beyond the risk of being thrown off course by those bumps. That makes *us* more free, and it also creates a free space for *others*, who no longer experience the tension of our hidden 'Don't touch!' notices.

Some bomb disposal techniques

My own inner furniture suffered some bruising one evening, as I well remember, during a discussion on Thomas Merton, who, as you may know, was a spiritual giant, whom I much admire, and also a vowed religious, but who broke his vows when in later life he fell in love. Something in this incongruity struck a raw nerve in me that I didn't realise was there. In no time at all, the discussion became disordered and unproductive as I, and others, groped around in the inner darkness of our mixed reactions, trying to put our 'furniture' back to rights. My own over-reaction so troubled me that I shared it with a spiritual director, who helped me to get to the root of my own disturbance about the subject, and also to realise that my re-action had a good deal more to do with *me*, than with Thomas Merton.

It happened, however, that only a few weeks later, someone spoke with me about a personal dilemma that also had strong connections with 'the Thomas Merton affair'. Though I wasn't conscious of it at the time, I realised, afterwards, that while listening to this person's story I had not experienced any inner turmoil of my own, but had been able to give my undivided and untroubled attention to them. This, I now know, would not have been possible if I hadn't been through the experience in the discussion group. As it was, I had already encountered this particular piece of inner furniture, and was no longer thrown by someone bumping into it again.

I share this with you only to assure you that it really does work:

- When you have recognised, and acknowledged, an item of your own inner furniture, you will not be thrown when someone bumps into it.
- This will make you more free.
- It will also create a free space for others, who will realise, sub-consciously, that this issue is no longer a 'no-go' area, and they will feel inwardly safe in opening it up with you.

If you find it difficult to imagine the difference between 'safe' and 'unsafe' space in another person's response to you, perhaps you have met one of those 'prickly people' who seem always to need handling with great care. These are the sort of people with whom you find yourself thinking, or even saying to yourself (and your children!): 'Whatever you do, don't mention such-and-such'. The taboo subjects can grow into a long list with some people – most of us have come across them! Now take your thoughts one step further and notice how you react to such people. I suggest that you will discover that you are very wary about what you talk about with them, and, in extreme cases, you may start to avoid them altogether, because they seem to be surrounded by a ring of invisible barbed wire.

All this tends to happen at a level below normal everyday awareness. One way into it is to notice your own *over-reactions*. These may well be pointing, as they were with me, to an area of tension inside you. If you can get in touch with the roots of this tension, possibly with the help of an understanding friend, you will go a long way towards defusing it. And others may have reason to be very grateful for your land-mine clearance operation, because it will increase the 'safe space' within *you*, where they may now safely venture.

Consolation and desolation – how to recognise them

Most of our feelings of desolation and of consolation can be traced back to the kind of roots we have been looking at in this chapter, but how do they show themselves in practice? The picture on the next page sums up the main symptoms of desolation, and the most commonly-experienced blessings of consolation. You may find it helpful to look back again over the moods of the past twenty-four hours and see whether you recognise any of these symptoms or have experienced any of these blessings.

In whatever ways we have ourselves experienced 'consolation' and felt ourselves, however briefly, to be close to God, these are moments to thank him for wholeheartedly, and moments to cherish in memory and return to deliberately when we find ourselves in periods of 'desolation', as a child returns to its parent's arms when things get difficult and bewildering in the outside world. To help us remember, it is good to write down our feelings at times of consolation and keep our memories accessible in this way.

Consolation is not the same as 'happiness'. It is possible to be in consolation, and very close to God, at times of real objective pain. I personally remember the two or three weeks of vigil as my mother was dying of cancer as a time of unusual closeness to God. Similarly, consolation can often give rise to tears. There is a big difference between tears of consolation and tears of desolation. Take a moment to recall how it feels when you have wept tears of desolation, winding yourself down ever more deeply into despair, and when you have felt so overwhelmed with joy, or with a sense of the presence of God, that your heart has filled up and overflowed in inexplicable tears, which were the tears of consolation.

Turns us in on ourselves.

Drives us down the spiral ever deeper into our own negative feelings.

Cuts us off from community.

Makes us want to give up on the things that used to be important to us.

Takes over our whole consciousness and crowds out our distant vision.

Covers up all our landmarks.

Drains us of energy.

Directs our focus outside and beyond ourselves.

Lifts our hearts so that we can see the joys and sorrows of other people.

Bonds us more closely to our human community.

Generates new inspiration and ideas.

Restores balance and refreshes our inner vision.

Shows us where God is active in our lives and where he is leading us.

Releases new energy in us.

Another useful test to apply to our moods is this: in a particular situation, am I feeling *drawn*, powerfully maybe, but always gently, or am I feeling *driven*? To get in touch with the difference between these feelings, we can recall times when someone has asked us to do something, for example, and reflect on our response: Did we say 'Yes' because we felt we really, deep down, *wanted* to do it, or did we go along with it to please someone else or to avoid conflict, but *against* our deeper inclinations? The action of God on our lives is always, at its heart, experienced as a *drawing*. If we are feeling driven, then the prompting that gives rise to it is not from

God, but from the force-fields of our own (or other people's) kingdoms. Ignatius compares consolation to the action of water falling softly onto a sponge, and desolation to the action of water splashing onto stone.

DRAWN or DRIVEN? Which do you feel?
God draws and the devil drives...

God's Kingdom

SOAKING or
SPLASHING?
Which do you feel?

my kingdom

If it saturates you
like a sponge, it is
probably from God...

If it splutters and clatters
it probably comes from your own
kingdom or from someone else's...

The picture below shows what consolation and desolation do to the innermost space of our hearts, or our 'WHO' centre. When I find my heart shrinking and sinking and turning to lead, like the figure in the picture, I often repeat to myself, like a mantra, the words: 'Lift up your hearts: we lift them to the Lord!' You may like to find some phrase or image that helps you at times like these to check the downward spiral of desolation. My daughter has given me a visual aid for this exercise – a little red wooden heart that tilts up and down at the end of a green stick. It sits next to my alarm clock, and helps me remember Who has given me the new day that I feel inclined to complain about!

Shrivels and shrinks your heart and makes it so heavy that it sinks to the lowest point of your experience.

Expands your heart until it is big enough to contain other people and their needs, and makes it light enough to fly to God.

LIFT UP YOUR HEARTS!
We (will try to) lift them up to the Lord!

The feelings and moods of the day, that we have been tracking, are about the kind of consolation and desolation that we all experience in every day we live. Sometimes, however, a wave of consolation seems to sweep over us for no apparent reason. It comes as a gratuitous gift from God (like all consolation), but it has the power to bowl us over. There are moments like these in Scripture, especially in the Gospels and in Acts. And we may be able to see the presence of such encounters in our own lives. Ignatius calls this experience 'consolation without previous cause' because it has no apparent trigger. Such an experience can only be received and welcomed in all humility. Often it seems to be given not to the most 'deserving' but to the most needy and the most unlikely recipients. It can never be 'achieved' and should not be looked for. Those who know such an experience often say, with hindsight, that it appears to have come just before a very difficult and challenging time in their lives, seemingly as a preparation and a strengthening for what lay ahead.

Consolation and the 'feelgood factor'

It isn't always obvious that there is a difference between experiencing spiritual consolation and simply 'feeling good', or finding oneself in spiritual desolation, and simply 'feeling low'. The effects can be very similar, but in fact the source is quite different.

To understand this fundamental difference, we really do need to notice the *direction of our attention*, as we go through the experience. The 'feelgood factor', as cultivated by politicians in particular, and its counterpart of 'feeling low' is intrinsically focused on ourselves. Things happen, in our own kingdoms, which trigger these ups and downs. In national terms, a reduction in taxation, for example, is supposed to 'lift our hearts'. At home, a family row can pitch us into the depths. If we could see the way our feelings are directed, we would notice that they are pointing in towards ourselves, and the satisfaction or disruption of our own personal worlds. This is completely natural, of course, and it is part of what makes us human. However, it can, as we know, be very easily deliberately manipulated, or affected by such things as our changing body chemistry, or how well we slept last night. These swings are not at all the same thing as spiritual consolation or desolation.

And the difference seems to lie in the *focus* of the experience. Spiritual consolation is experienced when our hearts are drawn towards God, even if, as we have seen, this happens in circumstances that 'the world' would regard as negative. It is a signal that our hearts, at least for that moment, are beating in harmony with the heart of God. Consolation is the experience of this deep connectedness to God, and it fills our being with a sense of peace and joy. The epicentre of the experience lies in God, and not in ourselves.

The reverse is true of spiritual desolation. This is felt when our hearts are turned away from God. A common pattern of desolation might look like this:

- Something happens in my life that upsets my 'kingdom'. Perhaps a desire of mine is frustrated, or something wounding is said or done to me.
- I *react* to the event by *focusing on my own pain*. This has the effect of turning my attention away from God and onto myself.
- I then find myself, as it were, standing with my back to the light, and seeing only my own shadow. As a result, the world appears dark and threatening.
- I can then all too easily imagine worse and worse consequences of the original negative event, and so I spiral down into deeper and deeper layers of desolation.

If we can learn to recognise these patterns, we can turn the negative movement round. The same unpleasant event may occur, but we can choose to react to it by trying to focus outwards, Godwards, instead of inwards upon our own pain. (This is by no means easy, and is only possible if our deep desire to move closer to God is actually stronger than the feeling of pain the event has caused in us. We will look more closely at this problem in a later chapter.)

When this begins to happen, we may experience a real breakthrough, leading to the discovery that God is actually drawing us closer to him through the very event that appears (at the 'WHERE' level of ourselves) to be so destructive.

This turning, or re-focusing, is a kind of ongoing, day-by-day, hour-by-hour conversion. Such 'turnings' are often invisible to anyone but ourselves and God, yet they can be more costly, more truly authentic and more likely to lead towards lasting change, than the more dramatic 'Damascus' experiences. Every day of our lives will bring its own share of 'little dyings', and in this sense we are called to a re-birth every time we react by turning towards God, instead of in upon ourselves. To be 'born again' is truly a continuous process.

One last word about consolation and desolation, before we move on, in the next chapter, to consider ways of using our moods to help us find our way in the dark. Our moods, as we know to our cost, are highly infectious.

How often have we clouded the hearts of our whole family or community by infecting them with our desolation, and how often have we felt ourselves being drawn down the deadly spiral of another person's desolation? On the other hand, next time you are driving to town on a sunny morning, notice how many of your fellow drivers are smiling, or singing to the car radio, or eager to acknowledge your courtesy if you give them the right of way! And notice what that does to your own mood.

Consolation and desolation are infectious, and yet, perversely, the advice in the picture is: 'Don't keep them to yourself!'

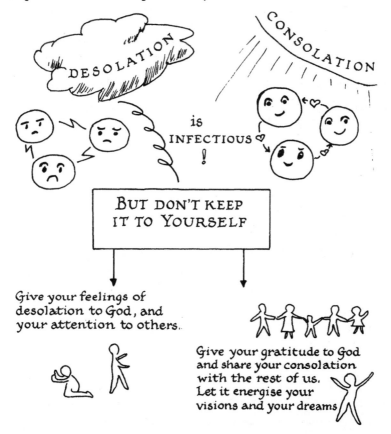

Desolation will choke you, so give your *feelings* over to God (not as easy as it sounds, but keep doing it anyway!), and turn your *attention* away from yourself and towards other people. Consolation will make you want to overflow with joy, so share your feelings with others, let the energy that consolation generates fuel your dreams and visions, and say Thankyou to God.

You might like to end this chapter by staying, in prayer, with a specific moment or period of consolation that you recall, and asking God to show you how to respond to it in a way that makes it a seed of growth for yourself, and for others.

5: THE NETTLE-BED AND THE ROSE-GARDEN
Suggestions for prayer and reflection

Try reflecting back over the past twenty-four hours (or a longer period if you wish), using the *Review of Consciousness* prayer. The guidelines in '*My Day With God: An evening prayer*' on page 95 may help you to notice where God has been present to you in the events and encounters of the day.

❀

In stillness, take the time to notice especially the *moods* of this past day. Have you experienced *Nettle-Bed* feelings at all? If so, can you trace their roots? What was really at the heart of the hurting? Have you spent any time in the *Rose-Garden*? Remember those moments and thank God for them. Then try to notice where they had their roots. Let your gratitude for those nourishing roots come to the surface. Thank God for them, and remember in your prayer any people, dead or alive, who have nourished your good roots.

❀

Take time to look inside your 'inner rooms'. Is there any 'furniture' standing there? Are there any 'Don't touch!' notices? Has anybody bumped into your furniture recently? How did it feel? Did it surprise you? What did it reveal to you about your invisible furniture? Have you bumped into anyone else's furniture?

❀

Has anyone infected you today with their desolation? Or their consolation? How did you react to it? How did it leave you feeling? Do you think that you yourself infected anyone else, either with desolation or consolation?

꽃

Reflect on any situation in your life where you are feeling *driven*. Who or what is doing the driving? Do you want it to be like that? If the situation troubles you, bring it to God now in prayer and show him how you are feeling. Let him lead you gently towards an understanding of the forces that are driving you, and where they have their source. Ask him to free you from any repeating patterns of 'drivenness' that you are experiencing.

Now reflect on those aspects of your life where you feel you are being *drawn*. How do they feel? Peaceful? Challenging? Exciting? Frightening? Try to describe them to yourself. Bring them to God in your prayer and let him show you where these things have their source. Let him affirm and strengthen those responses and feelings in you that have their origins in his guiding of your life.

꽃

Choose a phrase, or mantra, or an image for yourself that you feel would help you when you find yourself spiralling down into desolation. Maybe a phrase from scripture or from a favourite book or poem, or an endearment, or a name for God, a warm memory, a much-loved scene. Whatever you choose, store it away for yourself, 'for a rainy day'.

My Day With God: An evening prayer

The day is drawing to a close. Work, family, chores, children, life itself have filled every moment. Or perhaps the day was empty, long and lonely. There may have been no time, or inclination, for 'prayer', but there has been plenty of time, and space, for God.

Where was he? How was he?

This prayerful reflection, which can be made in as little as ten minutes, has been used for centuries by countless believers. It can help to draw your day together and open your eyes to the intricate and beautiful patterns of light, shade and colour, that the Lord has been weaving through the fabric of your minutes and your hours.

The pattern of the prayer is like this:

Stillness. Relax; be still, let the tensions of the day slip away from you. Know that you are in God's presence. He rejoices that you have come to him, however forgetful you may have been of him during the day.

Thankfulness. Remember with thanksgiving the gifts of God to you today. A meeting with a friend; a glimpse of deep joy or sadness in a passing face; a flower at the wayside; a baby's first steps; a grandparent's smile; a friendly shop assistant; a considerate driver; a moment of insight; a job done; a problem solved; a child's hug; a lover's touch; a warm memory; a rising moon; a falling leaf . . . Be still, in the memory, and offer God your thanks in your own way.

Light-seeking. Ask God to help you see and understand how his love has been working within you today. This is a gift of the Spirit and it has been promised to all who sincerely seek it.

Reflection. Reflect peacefully on what has been happening to you and in you today, trusting that your prayer for the light of his Spirit has been granted. Let him show you whatever he may want to show you. The questions that follow are only suggestions to prompt your reflection. If you feel drawn to a particular question, stay with it and let God speak to your heart about it:

- How were you drawn to God today: a friend, the beauty of nature, a book, a letter, a gentle thought?
- Have you learned anything today about God and his ways, in the everyday events of living and in the world around you?
- Did you meet him in: fears, joys, work, misunderstandings, weariness, pain? (One way of meeting God is to recognise our *need* of him.)

- Did his word come alive for you in prayer, in Scripture, in liturgy, in his creation?
- Did you bring Christ to those around you? Did they bring him to you?
- Have you been a sign of God's presence and love to the people you met today? Did you come across someone who was lonely, sad, discouraged or in need; did you recognise the need in their eyes; did you respond?
- Did you sense the presence of God in the wider world, perhaps in what you saw on TV or read in the papers. Can you bring him your feelings – your anger, your compassion?
- Did anything happen today to make you feel loved? Were you able to show love to another person today?
- Did you feel the absence of God in any part of your day? If so, why do you think that was?
- How were your moods today? What made you feel peaceful? Where did you experience unease or even turmoil? Reflect on what it was that seemed to cause you to react with these feelings, and open them up to God, for affirmation or for healing.
- Did you feel God calling you, prompting you, nudging you in any particular way today? How did you respond?
- Out of all your day's experience, is there one special incident or discovery that you would like to thank him for?

Sorrow. With hindsight you may realise that much of your reaction to the events of the day has been centred on your own 'kingdom'. This may have led you to fail to respond to the cry of another person, or to allow your own pre-occupations to take centre stage and crowd out other people's needs. Your day may have left little space for an awareness of God or of his creation. Whatever inadequacies you find in your day's living, let them be there before God now, not for judgement, but for his Spirit to hover over the mess, bringing wholeness out of brokenness, as once that same Spirit brought creation out of chaos. Express your sorrow to God, and confidently ask for his healing and forgiveness.

Hopefulness. Look forward to tomorrow. Ask him to open your heart to whatever surprises it may bring; to open your eyes to notice him in unexpected places; to open your ears to become tuned in to the unceasing song of his kingdom. Pray for the sensitivity to recognise the Lord in whatever ways he may greet you and call you. Something of God lies still concealed for you in tomorrow's journey. Look forward to discovering it.

Even if there is no other chance for prayer during your day, try to form the habit of reviewing your day quietly in this way each evening (or at some other appropriate time). You will quickly find that you start to look out for God's presence and his action in places you would not have thought to look before. And his promise is sure ... *those who seek him will find him.*

6. THE INNER COMPASS

Finding our way in the dark

We recall, because it is crucially important, that because the general orientation of our lives is *towards* God, our feelings of consolation will point us towards *his* action in our lives, and our feelings of desolation will, in general, warn us that it is the things of our own kingdom that are dominating our attention.

How, then, can we use these feelings to help us find our way on the inner journey?

This chapter will look at two images that may help us: the image of the inner compass, and the image of the stars.

Most of us have grown up with an uncomfortable awareness that life presents us with endless opportunities for falling into error and into sin, and we have a vague sense that some of these sins and errors are more serious in their consequences than others. Our attempts to negotiate these hurdles can feel like trying to cross a minefield. We can find ourselves thinking that if we only knew where all these mines were buried, we would know how to get to heaven without mishap. As it is, however, we spend our spiritual energy trying to hit an invisible dartboard and we wonder why we get frustrated!

Of course, all this is a playful caricature, yet it has uncomfortable grains of truth. Many of us, if challenged, would find that we cherish the notion of 'God's Will' as something that is fixed in stone somewhere, and our task in life is to discover it and to do it. The purpose of this chapter is to look at this limited understanding, and see how we can get in touch with the nature of 'God's Will' more creatively and effectively, with the help of our moods and feelings. For it is there, buried in our feelings and our moods, that we can actually notice, at a real and personal level, the inner movements of our hearts, and the roots of our desires and resistances, and, by grace, allow our lives to be drawn into deeper harmony with God and with our own truest centre. This process then begins to look much less like aiming, blindfold, at an invisible dartboard, and much more like the gradual, steady, certain evolution of a beautiful flower from its first beginnings in the seed.

But how do we find our way through the unmapped terrain of our lives and of our hearts' desires and conflicts? Especially when the fogs of desolation descend on us? You might like to have a look at two 'tools' that I have found helpful myself in finding my way.

The inner compass: where is it and how do I use it?

Those of you who have done any hill-walking will know how rapidly the clouds can come down and leave you stranded in impenetrable fog. When that happens, the guidebooks you have carefully packed in your rucksack become useless, because you can't see any landmarks and the temptation is to try to resolve the problem by effort and activity, with the result that you go round in circles, and if you are on dangerous ground, you may well fall down a crevasse or off a cliff.

A very similar thing happens to us spiritually, when desolation descends on us. We lose our distant vision and our consciousness fills up entirely with the immediate problem, whatever it is (and it may well be something that appears to be good, but is actually becoming obsessive). All the useful books we have read and sermons we have listened to lose their meaning, because we can't find anything to relate them to in our immediate lived experience. And our instinctive response to all of this is to go into frantic mental activity, to 'solve' the problem, or at the very least to find someone to blame for it. We quickly find ourselves going round in circles. If we are in any serious kind of trouble, there is a real risk of a dangerous fall.

It is at this point when, if we are wise, on the mountains we will turn to the compass. If we know how to use it, it will show us the way, however thick the fog. To use it, we need first of all to know where it is. It needs to be readily accessible in the rucksack, and not twenty miles away in the youth hostel, for one thing. And we need to know how to use it in conjunction with the map. And, most essential, to use it, we need to stand still, and let the needle come to rest.

How do these skills relate to our inner compass? Remarkably the same,

I believe. We need to know how to access it – that is, we need to be in touch with, and at home with our moods, and skilled in recognising consolation and desolation and responding accordingly. This skill needs to be ready and primed in our hearts, and not twenty miles away in our heads! We can develop this skill, with God's help, in prayer, and especially in the review of consciousness prayer that we looked at in the previous chapter.

Secondly, we need to use the compass along with the map on which the record of our experience is laid out, in the way shown in the picture.

This map reflects our distant vision, from the times when we *could* see it because the weather was clear. These were the times of consolation to which we must return when the clouds are down. When we place the compass on the map of our truest experience, it will reliably show us the direction we should take now that we are temporarily blinded to our destination and to the familiar landmarks.

And finally, to use this tool, which we call *discernment*, we must come to stillness. In the silence of our hearts and our prayer, we must wait patiently for the compass needle to steady into stillness. Then it will point to true north, the still centre, the '*fine point of the soul*', and we will be enabled to move forward again.

There is only one more thing necessary, and this is perhaps the most difficult part of all: we must *trust* the compass. How many of us hill walkers have gone through all the procedure of taking our bearings on a fogbound summit, only to decide afterwards that our own defective memories and instincts are more reliable than the compass and to follow them instead. I have done that myself, and ended up in completely the wrong valley at the end of the day. I don't want to take a chance like that on my spiritual journey!

You're going to need your inner compass!

Where is it?	It needs to be in your heart and not your head.
Can you use it?	It needs practice ~ prayer and reflection are your practice.
Is it steady?	Can you come to inner stillness, so that God can show you the movements of your heart?
Do you trust it?	Your heart shows you the way. Don't get into arguments with your head!

Walking by the stars

So, the inner compass is a tool for the fogbound days, as well as being a great help when the sun shines and the way ahead seems clear, and we are noticing the landmarks and signs that compose our inner map. Another way of plotting our course is by the stars. It always fascinates me to reflect that if we could hurtle through space, we would not see any constellations. As it is, when we stand still at any point on earth, beneath a clear night sky, we see these familiar patterns.

Two things are worth bearing in mind about these constellations. First, they never look quite the same from two different viewing points. Two near neighbours would see the constellations in very slightly different perspective. Two people at opposite sides of the world would see a completely different set of pictures in the heavens. Our personal view depends on where we are standing. Secondly, the constellations are not the reality of the stars, but only the pattern we impose upon them, in order to recognise them, use them to find our bearings, and talk to each other about them.

What can the constellations tell us about our inner pathfinding? I believe that when we come to stillness before God, when we let that coming-to-stillness become a habit, and when we begin to live reflectively, learning to recognise the patterns of our consolations and desolations, we begin to see the personal inner constellations of our experience that can guide us. These may be clusters of fear and anxieties to which we are particularly prone, or areas of special giftedness in our lives, ways of praying that seem consistently to bring us closer to God, aspects of our way of relating to others that tend to have destructive effects. Whether negative or positive, these personal patterns of being can be invaluable aids in steering our course in the dark. And it is significant that the stars do only shine in the dark. The dark areas of our experience can be the very places where we discover God most plainly. The picture overleaf suggests a way of looking at this.

Like the heavenly constellations, the patterns we discover are not the reality of ourselves, but only helpful indicators of our inner movements, by which we might locate ourselves and feel our way forward, remembering all the time that every other person's interior night sky will be different from, but no less valid than, our own.

As a practical exercise, in prayer, we might ask God to lead us to the discovery of the constellations that help our journey and try to identify one cluster of gifts in ourselves, and one cluster of fears. With this knowledge in our hearts, we can use our discernment to nurture the gifts and seek freedom from the tyranny of the fears.

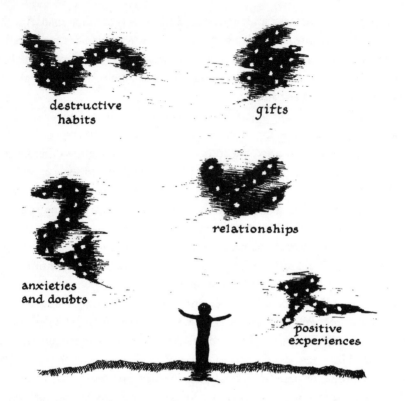

destructive
habits

gifts

relationships

anxieties
and doubts

positive
experiences

Staying on course

And so, we have some equipment for our inner journey. We have the gift of discernment, our inner compass, which will show us more and more clearly and reliably where our personal True North lies – that is, in what parts of our experience, and especially in our prayer experience, we are most truly centred on, and directed towards, God. And we have our inner constellations, which show us where our clusters of desolation and consolation are most likely to be encountered. Both these gifts are given uniquely to each individual, and each of us is personally responsible to God for developing and using them, and empowered to do so by God's indwelling spirit at our centre.

However, although we are walking our own unique way with God, we are also making a journey that has been made by countless pilgrim feet before us, and Ignatius gives us some signposts on the route. The next picture offers some general guidelines on how to proceed:

- When the clouds of desolation are down and you can't see your own nose in front of you, or,
- When the sun is smiling and you can't imagine why you ever had a problem!

WARNING! DESOLATION!
1. Tell God how you feel and ask for help.
2. Seek out companionship.
3. Don't go back on decisions you made in consolation.
4. Stand still and remember your inner map.
5. Recall a time of consolation and go back to it in imagination.
6. Look for someone who needs your help and turn your attention towards them.
7. Go back to 1.

WELCOME! CONSOLATION!
1. Tell God how you feel & thank him.
2. Store this moment in your memory to return to when things get tough.
3. Add this experience to your life map.
4. Use the energy you feel to further your deepest desires.
5. Let the surplus energy fuel the things you don't like doing, and do them.
6. Go back to 1.

Keep these instructions safely with your inner compass – that is, engraved on your heart! Apply the Desolation Rules whenever your inner compass starts to spin. Reflect on the Consolation Rules when your compass needle is reading True North.

And if the worst happens, and the fog gets so thick that you really can't move an inch, try using the tactics shown in this picture:

When desolation roots you to the spot,
cut free from the desolating currents, by
ACTING AGAINST THEM...

- Tell God, and maybe a human friend, how you feel and ask them to prise you away from the negative force fields, even though you really want to stay where you are, in isolation.
- Force yourself to make contact with other people; go to town, walk round the market, make yourself a meal, phone a friend, even though you don't feel like doing any of these things.
- Do 'just one thing' that needs doing (perhaps some small practical task), and then enjoy the satisfaction of having done it. Give yourself a pat on the back, then look for the next 'one thing'.
- Make a deliberate effort to reach out to the need of another person, maybe someone with similar difficulties, even though you really don't want to know about anyone else right now.
- Pick up a project that really fired your imagination when you were in consolation. Let it refresh you with positive energy, even though you don't actually want to do anything at all.
- Stay with the decisions you made, the dreams you dreamed, when in consolation, even though you really feel like giving up on life.
- Remember moments of consolation, when God seemed close to you and re-enact them in your mind, even though you are tempted to dismiss them.

If real solid desolation gets hold of you, it operates like an electric shock and literally welds you to the spot. In this situation your concern is not for your inner progress, but solely and simply for your survival. It is likely that you won't get free of the desolating currents without help – certainly you will need God's help, and maybe that of a human friend as well, preferably one who knows what desolation can do to you. Your spiritual firefighters, in this situation, are like cutting equipment to get you free from the source of the paralysis.

You can help yourself by using the *Act Against It!* method. You could compare this survival technique with what the Jesuits call '*agere contra*' (to act against; to drive oneself against one's inclinations). I used to think this was a perverse form of discipline that stopped you doing everything you were good at and insisted on your doing the things you were bad at, for the sake of developing humility. Now, however, I discover in my own experience that this is far more than a dubious ascetic practice: it is a strategy for surviving *and overcoming* desolation and getting moving again on the journey home to wholeness.

And when I go astray?

You could be forgiven for feeling doubtful as to whether these methods are as reliable as they sound. After all, it remains a fact of our lives that, in spite of our discernment, and in spite of our self-knowledge about the constellations of our lives, we can rarely look back over a day and feel that we really have been travelling True North in all our actions and decisions.

When these thoughts take hold of me, I look up to the stars and ponder the shape of *The Plough*. When the conditions are right, and the night sky is clear, I do this literally and it has become one of my most powerful and sanity-restoring prayers. Look at the shape of the constellation of *The Plough*, in the picture on the next page.

This is the constellation that is used to locate the position of the Pole Star. If you start at the curly end of *The Plough* and follow it through until you reach the frying pan part, and then follow the line formed by the last two stars, for roughly two-and-a-half times their distance, you come to the Pole Star, and you are facing due North.

Try it out sometime, and relish the feeling, inwardly and outwardly, of standing facing True North, with your feet planted firmly in your own back yard. This is a real promise, and something to be trusted. Then look

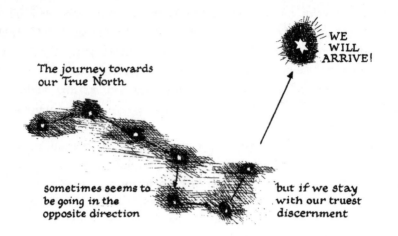

The journey towards
our True North

WE
WILL
ARRIVE!

sometimes seems to
be going in the
opposite direction

but if we stay
with our truest
discernment

at how you arrived there, all round the convoluted corners and kinks of the frying pan, including a period when you appeared to be travelling in precisely the opposite direction! When I see *The Plough*, I see the whole course of our human history and our quest for God, and I see my own little journey in there too, meandering wildly at times, but ultimately, and certainly, leading me home to where I truly AM.

6: THE INNER COMPASS: FINDING OUR WAY IN THE DARK
Suggestions for prayer and reflection

A starlight journey ...

After Jesus had been born at Bethlehem in Judaea during the reign of King Herod, some wise men came to Jerusalem from the east. 'Where is the infant king of the Jews?' they asked. 'We saw his star as it rose, and have come to do him homage.'. . .

Then Herod summoned the wise men to see him privately. He asked them the exact date on which the star had appeared, and sent them on to Bethlehem. 'Go and find out all about the child,' he said, 'and when you have found him, let me know, so that I too may go and do him homage.'

Having listened to what the king had to say, they set out. And there in front of them was the star they had seen rising; it went forward and halted over the place where the child was.

The sight of the star filled them with delight, and going into the house they saw the child with his mother Mary, and falling to their knees they did him homage. Then, opening their treasures, they offered him gifts of gold and frankincense and myrrh.

But they were warned in a dream not to go back to Herod, and returned to their own country by a different way.

(Matthew 2:2, 7–12)

Try to imagine yourself alongside these stargazers. Let the picture unfold to you. Recall the first sighting of that special star – your own Pole Star. Re-live the excitement of that discovery, and the certainty that this journey *must* be made, that it would lead you to the pearl of great price.

In prayer, make your own journey now, following that special star. Notice the landscape of your journey, your companions, the sights and sounds and smells of the countryside and the townships through which your journey leads you. Can you still see the star? How do you feel? What are you hoping for?

On your journey there are times of pure joy. Remember them. Thank God for them. And there are times when you feel threatened, as the Magi did. Can you name any of those times now and lay your feelings before God, exactly as they are, undisguised?

As your journey moves on, you gradually learn to discern between what can be trusted and what cannot. What has helped you make this discernment? When was your discernment right? When did it let you down? Can you see any reasons for this?

Now imagine your arrival. Your Pole Star has come to rest above the place where your deepest desire lies. How do you react? Live the scene out now in your prayer and let your destination speak to you.

❀

Try drawing your own lifemap, showing the terrain of your innermost self. What are the paths that tend to lead you into desolation? And what is the landscape of your consolation like? What trees grow in your forest of gifts? Where are your prayer pools? Are they full and flowing or do they feel dry? What rivers feed into them, bringing you encouragement and grace?

There is no limit to what might appear on your lifemap. Populate it as you wish. It is for your eyes only.

❀

Now take a walk beneath the night sky. Let your prayer reveal to you your personal constellations, by which you can plot your course. Draw your own pictures, either in your mind or on paper, of the constellations and what they mean to you. You may like to use the ideas shown in the picture on page 104 as starting points, and then go on to add your own unique star-pointers – those things in your life that warn you that you are moving off-course, and those that affirm your direction as True North.

❀

Draw your own *Plough*. At what times in your life did your journey seem, with hindsight, to be leading you in the wrong direction? How do you feel about your direction now? Is there any way in which you would wish to correct your course? The shape of your journey might not look like the *Plough*. Try drawing the shape you feel your life is taking, maybe putting dates against crucial phases that you remember on your inner journey and naming significant events or people.

7. THE DEEPEST DESIRE

Desire is not easy to draw ... not easy to describe ... not easy to think about ... not easy to live with ...

Yet we are told that desire is the source of our vital energy, and that our inner journey is focused – consciously or unconsciously – on our *deepest desire*. It also seems to be the case that the coin of our deepest desire has a reverse face, where our deepest fear is imprinted.

What does desire mean for us? Is it really so crucially important? How do we come to terms, creatively, with this seething mass of conflicting needs and hopes, dreams, dreads and longings that we find in our hearts?

In this chapter we will not be seeking definitions or explanations. Instead I will share with you a few pictures that have helped me to get in touch with my deepest desires, and that I hope may strike a chord with you too.

The thrust of our desiring

Desire is a *strong* word, full of energy. When we encounter our desires, we know that we are dealing with something forceful. '*Thrust*' seems the right word. Desires force themselves into our consciousness, whether we invite and encourage them or whether we try to bar our mental doors against them. If we suppress them, they simply go underground, like bramble roots, and surface somewhere else, when we least expect them. We don't need to be depth psychologists to recognise the power of this phenomenon in our lives.

It all reminds me of the thrust of growth we find in nature. A tree shows what I mean.

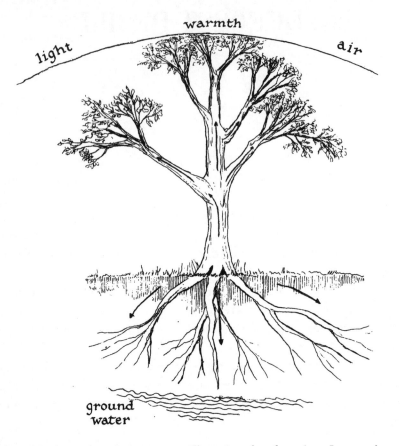

If you look at the picture you will notice the thrusting. It goes in two directions. The life-force inside the tree thrusts roots deep down into the ground, seeking water and nutrients. And at the same time the above-ground growth is thrusting branches out into the air, seeking the light and warmth of the sun and the life-giving components of the air. In the downward thrust of its roots, the tree obtains its firm hold in the earth, and its nourishment. In the upward thrust of its branches it reaches for light and warmth but it also *expresses*, in a visible form, the truth and beauty of its own unique being.

It seems to me that our desires are quite a lot like that. When I look at the nature of my own desires I see these two directions of thrust:

• Desires that delve deep down, seeking hold and nourishment and security. Let me call these my *root desires.*

- Desires that urge me to express myself, to spread out my arms and my heart to the world around me and to my friends and loved ones; to reach out to those things that embody light and warmth for me – those things that *delight* me and warm my heart. I could call these my *branch desires*.

A few examples might help to clarify this picture.

Among my *root desires* I find such things as:

- A desire for safety and comfort; a desire for a stable home and a peaceful world in which I can be rooted.
- A desire for physical, mental and spiritual nourishment.
- A desire to belong to a network of loving and accepting friends, who hold me in equilibrium even when outer circumstances get difficult.
- A thirst always to go deeper, for example in friendship, in study, in prayer.

And among my *branch desires* I find:

- A desire to do work that is creative, that expresses the 'real me' in the outside world.

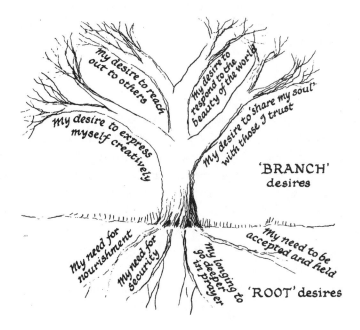

- A desire to express, to trusted friends, the deepest feelings and hopes and dreams of my heart.
- A desire to show my compassion when I meet someone in distress, to open my heart towards them.
- A desire somehow to go 'outside' and 'beyond' myself, when I am deeply moved, for example by a piece of music, or a starlit night.

You might like to reflect on your own root and branch desires. The picture on page 128 may help you to focus your reflections. Try to be specific as far as you can. This will 'ground' your desires and help you get in touch with the real, tangible, incarnate nature of them; the exercise is only valuable if it reveals *actual* desires, not abstract concepts.

We could say that one thing our desires do for us is to prove that the universe (or even our own personal world) is not centred on ourselves. There is something *beyond*, towards which our living energy is always striving. Delving down for security, stability, peace, nourishment, encouragement, companionship, intimacy. Reaching out for creative self-expression, for the joy of responding to other forms of creativity, for fruitfulness and expansiveness. The tree roots go deep because there is always something deeper to strive for. Its branches reach up because the sky, the sun and the air are always beyond and out of reach.

Yet it is precisely in the striving that the growth and the fruitfulness happen. It is in our seeking that we are found.

Identifying our deepest desire

By now you are probably well aware of the kind of desires that are milling around in your own heart, and you have perhaps been able to name them specifically, and recognise something of their nature, and of your own ways of responding to them. However, this still seems a long way from being able to recognise where these desires have their deepest roots. We all know the experience of desire, and the certainty that if and when we attain what we desire, we will still remain, at a deep level, unsatisfied.

St Augustine expresses this feeling: 'Our souls are restless, Lord, until they find their rest in you.'

It's as if every desire that we can experience and name points *beyond* itself. And where is that 'beyond'? Well, we will surely not, in our human form, be able to reach out to that ultimate 'beyond', but our deepest desire will bring us, perhaps, as close to it as the human spirit might venture. Most importantly, we will discover that we find our deepest desire not in our *arriving*, but in our *journeying*; not in the *finding*, but in the *searching*. 'Seek, and you will find' (or rather, you will *be found*, by the One who is seeking *you*) in the very heart of the searching.

And how, in practice, might we come to recognise those deep desires that touch the heart of our being? I would like to share two practical methods with you. These might be called: *Outside In*, and *Inside Out*, respectively. The *Outside In* method begins with the desires we *know* we have, or have had, in our conscious living. The *Inside Out* method begins rather in the depths of ourselves with desires that we have only dimly sensed, but never named, and to which we have access via myth and fairy story.

Outside In

In the *Outside In* method, we recall some of the desires that have dominated our hearts at different times of our lives. I have called it *Outside In* because it starts with the desires we know we have, or have had at different times, and leads us deeper into the underlying longings that these desires are expressing.

I remember, for example, when I was thirteen, desperately longing for a dog, and for a bike. These desires were more than just 'Christmas wish list' desires; they had something of driving passion in them. What was it? It helps me to understand what it was when I recall how I felt when my parents did indeed buy a puppy, and gave me a second-hand bike for my fourteenth birthday. At first I was delighted, but, ultimately, the deep desire I had felt remained still somehow unfulfilled, and was displaced by the next heart-dream. So if the puppy and the bike were not the real roots of those desires, what was?

Now, in prayer and with hindsight, I can see that in the puppy I was more deeply seeking companionship for a lonely childhood and this was partially fulfilled, and in the bike the real desire was for a new degree of freedom and independence and this too was partially fulfilled. Yet the days came when there *was* real human companionship and there *was* full adult independence. And still I remain unfulfilled. Still I haven't fully grasped the root of my deepest desire.

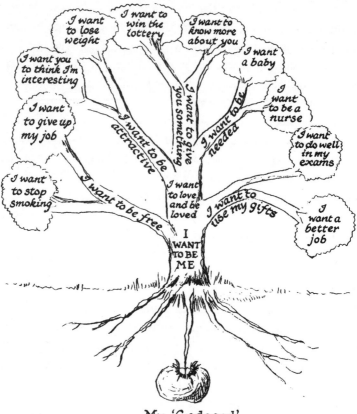

My 'Godseed'

Take a moment to reflect on any desires that you can identify like this, perhaps from childhood, or in careers or relationships. The picture shows how our desires, like our moods, have deep hidden roots, and if we follow these roots to their first origins (given that our directedness is towards God) will we not discover that all our deeply-felt desires, at their true source, will be connected with our desire for God himself and our desire to become the person he is dreaming into being in our Who-centre?

What is it that we are really longing for, and never quite find? And do we, perhaps, begin to find it in those moments when we experience the deep peace and solidity of consolation? Perhaps we begin to find it when we begin to notice God gradually unfurling his reality in our own Who-centre.

Inside Out

The *Inside Out* method offers us a rather different way of getting in touch with our own deepest desires, and, indeed, with the deepest desires and longings that seem to run through all human experience, and in which we find our own dreams located. This is the method of *fairy-tale*. Absurd though it may appear at first sight, we can begin to get in touch with our own heart-dreams simply by picking up one of those discarded fairy story books that we once read to our children or grandchildren, or that we still cherish from our own childhood.

I have called this the *Inside Out* method because fairy stories take us right to the heart of our desiring, by the way of pictures, symbols and metaphors, and help us to connect these deep and universal desires (and fears) to the feelings we are experiencing ourselves, in our particular circumstances.

To try this method, sit back and relax and let your memory rove over the fairy tales that come to mind from your childhood. Does a particular favourite story come to mind? You may like to bring it into prayer, by consciously asking God to show you what its meanings are telling you about your own desires and about *his* desire for *you*.

As an example, we could look together at a few types of story. The first type is the '*Becoming who I really am*' story, and we can see this meaning in, for example, the story of the Ugly Duckling or Cinderella. Is there an ugly duckling in you? Have you glimpsed the swan? Do you feel drawn to ask God to 'grow' you from the duckling you feel like now to the swan you dream of becoming in him?

A second type of story is the '*Free me from the evil spell*' story. We can see this in such tales as Sleeping Beauty. These stories give us inner space in which to experience the coming of the Prince who recognises our deepest needs and feels such compassion and love for us that he will risk his life to set us free from the spell that binds us and leaves us helpless to help ourselves. You might like to take such a story into your prayer and let God speak his personal word to you there. He may be waiting for an opportunity to convince you how much he loves you, or to reveal to you the seriousness of the spell that holds you, or even to engage your co-operation in taking risks to free others from their spells.

Then there is the '*Just One Wish*' story. Think, for example, of King

Midas who wished that everything he touched might turn to gold. Ponder before God, what you would wish for if you could ask God to grant you just one of your desires. What is this one wish showing you about the things you are most deeply hoping and longing for in your life? Let yourself be Cinderella and receive your fairy godmother into your imagination. What ball do you want to go to? And why do you want to go so much?

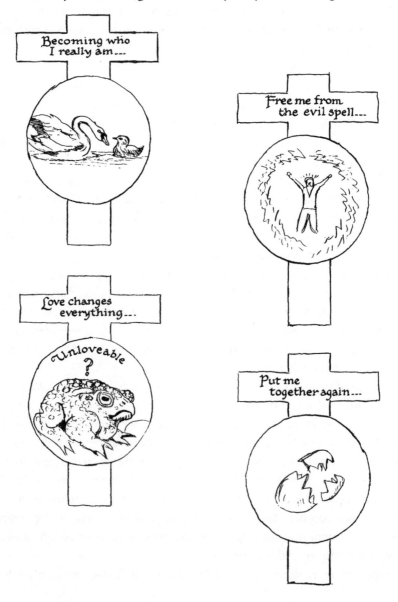

For a good night out? To get your own back on the ugly sisters in your life? Or because you feel drawn towards the possibility of real and lasting transformation?

And finally, perhaps the most powerful story of all, that we find, for example, in The Frog Prince. This is the '*Love Changes Everything*' story. Do you feel like a frog most of the time? Deep down are you inclined to think that no-one would really like you if they really knew you? Now let the princess rest her all-knowing gaze upon you. Let her give you the transforming kiss, however hard, however impossible it feels. Let yourself be loved by the only one who really knows you, because he made you for his own.

All this sounds like news that is far too good to be true! And, yes, the fears and shadows that lurk around our hearts are not dismissed by the wave of a magic wand. There is, inevitably, a Humpty Dumpty sitting precariously on the walls of our lives and likely to fall apart at any moment! And all our king's horses and all our king's men won't get us together again, whatever we do. At best we might manage a rather shell-shocked omelette. But what God promises is a chick pecking its way out of our broken shells to Something New!

In so many ways these familiar stories are gospel stories, with considerable power to reveal to us who we really are, and who we are longing to become. They occur in all cultures and languages, with remarkably similar detail, precisely because they are about the desires that lie at the roots of all human hoping and striving.

Confronting the But-Bird

These practical exercises may have helped you to recognise the patterns of your own desires – what you wish you were, what you wish you possessed, what you dream of doing or becoming – and the deeper underlying roots of these desires.

We go on now to consider what it is that seems to stop these desires from reaching fulfilment. Remember, we are talking here of the matters that stir our hearts at the deepest levels, not daydreams like 'I wish I could go to the moon, but I can't afford the fare.' An example may help: I have a colleague who is a very gifted amateur artist, but whose drawings were largely confined to the margins of his notepad, in the form of doodles during boring meetings. A number of people commented on his talent, but he always continued to put himself down. However, the invitations to him to 'draw something' began to multiply, from the parish magazine to a set of illustrations for a book. Just before the book went to press, he confided that it had been 'a lifelong dream' of his to illustrate a book. Yet he had never told anyone of this dream, not even, I suspect, himself. And he had never done anything actively to bring about its realisation. Why not?

What is it that stops us from acknowledging our dreams and seeking to fulfil them? Whatever the reasons in my colleague's case, a couple of general suggestions might be considered:

- We do not believe in ourselves, even though we say we believe in our Creator. We seem to harbour the notion that, although God declared his work to be 'good', we alone are 'rejects'. Sometimes, just announcing ourselves to be 'rubbish' isn't good enough; we have to be the 'worst rubbish of all'. But God doesn't, as someone once said, 'make junk'.
- We *do* believe in ourselves, deep down, but we are afraid that other people might not. We are afraid of exposing ourselves to public opinion. We are afraid to risk our 'talent' on the open market. And the fear is stronger than our desire to exercise our gifts fruitfully.

My desire to use my gifts

My fear of rejection and ridicule

My fears outweigh my desire,
My fears hold me down,
My fears refuse to let me grow,
to let me fly, to let me be ME!

Perhaps we can get to the root of our fears in the same way that we probed our desires. As a practical exercise, try looking back over the last twenty-four hours again. Were there any moments when you felt a sudden stab of anxiety about something? Was there something around during that period that seemed to be clouding you over with a sense of foreboding or worry? Perhaps something jumped inside you when the phone rang or there was a knock at the door. Perhaps you read something, heard a conversation, saw something on television that summoned up a wall of resistance in you. Maybe you were asked to do something or go somewhere, and you realised that the very thought of doing so brought you up against an inner brick wall. Or possibly, you felt an impulse to do something and then stopped yourself, thinking, 'I couldn't . . .' Ask God to show you what, or who, lay at the root of those feelings.

The positive energies

The negative energies

I want to be 'me' without masks or disguises
I want to write a poem
I want to say how I really feel
I want to do something different
I want to give you a present
I want to say 'I love you'

BUT

People might not like 'me'
you might laugh at me
I might destroy our friendship
I might lose my security
you might misunderstand my motives
you might reject me

The bird in my heart wants to fly,
    free and high,
but my fears clip its wings and keep
        it earthbound!

Where shall I align myself?
With the good or the bad spirits?
With the desires or the fears?
    With the positive or the negative energies?

In everything I do, I have a choice....!

As an example, let's consider the mother of a small child who goes out to a concert. She finds she isn't really enjoying the concert because she is worried about whether the child is all right, and whether the concert will finish in time for her to be home at the time she promised the baby-sitter. She is only aware of some general unease within herself, that is distracting her from the music. What might be at the root of it? Perhaps there are fears about her own judgement – is the baby-sitter reliable? Or about the relationship with her child – what if he wakes and finds me gone? Or maybe there are feelings of guilt about going out at all, or even about enjoying herself. Such fears could even be pointing to a damaging image of God as a figure of threat and punishment. Whatever they are, they are taking her over and undermining her enjoyment of the concert.

Our fears, then, are perhaps the worst enemies of our desires, as the picture on page 121 shows. If we could imagine them as sentient beings, we might come to the conclusion that they are waging a deliberate, lifelong campaign against the fulfilment of the God-dream in us, as it is expressed in our own deepest desires.

Ignatius calls such negative inner movements the *false spirits* inside us, and he calls the positive movements the *good spirits*. The discernment process is the ongoing task of learning to recognise when we are being driven by the false, negative, destructive spirits and when we are being drawn by the good, positive, creative spirits in our hearts. Once discernment is being practised, prayerfully, in the ways we have explored, it becomes possible, consciously, to start to feed the wholesome plants and stop watering the weeds. It also becomes possible to begin to make decisions with a greater degree of inner freedom.

7: THE DEEPEST DESIRE
Suggestions for prayer and reflection

> 'God, you are my God, I am seeking you,
> my soul is thirsting for you,.
> my flesh is longing for you,
> a land parched, weary and waterless.'

(Psalm 63:1)

Let these words soak into your heart, as you sit, silently relaxed, in God's presence. Imagine yourself as a sponge, soaking up God's love for *you*. Feel him filling your heart. Feel the living water trickling through the highways and the by-ways of your life – through your experience of living *today*.

Notice how you are feeling. Notice especially those parts of your being that feel 'worn-out and waterless'. How does the living water affect them? In your prayer, lay them open, without fear or disguise, to God, and express to him, in a way that feels right for *you*, your own response to him.

❦

Try drawing your own life-tree, like that in the picture on page 112, and name those feelings and longings in yourself that you would see as *root desires* and *branch desires*.

❦

Remember, if you can, one or two things in your life that you have really *longed* for. Can you identify now what deeper needs and longings lay beneath these desires?

❦

Do you have a favourite fairy story? If you do, remember it in your prayer, and re-live it in your imagination. Is it opening up a personal story in your heart? If so, let it become a 'gospel story' for you, like those shown on page 118.

❦

What secret dreams or ambitions do you cherish? What is it that prevents you from seeking to fulfil them? Try setting your dreams alongside the blocks which 'clip their wings'. Do you *want* to stay with the blocks? If not, how might you encourage the positive movements in your life more strongly? Bring your feelings and your fears into prayer.

❦

Write a short 'wish-list' of things you hope for right now (like those at the end of the branches in the picture on page 116). Try tracing these things back, to see which branch of your desires is supporting them and where they really have their origins.

8. WHY DON'T YOU ANSWER MY PRAYERS?

God's will and my desire

There was a time when I thought of my prayers as some kind of lottery. I might get lucky on a few of my scratchcard prayers and clock up a few ticks, as if I were checking God off against a shopping list. Big wins were a lot less likely – really only dreams. Some people even keep diaries of the answers they feel they have, or have not received to their specific prayers.

Today, though, I really question this way of thinking of prayer and the ways in which God responds to it. To explain what I mean, we need to go back to our thoughts on the 'deepest desire'. An image may help here. We could imagine our 'deepest desire' as a powerful underground stream. Indeed, there are many images of exactly such a stream in Scripture (for example, Ezekiel's stream, or Jesus' promise of the living water). This stream is so deep in our hearts that for the most part we are not even aware of it ourselves. Remember how difficult it was, really to get in touch with the deepest longings of our hearts, when we tried to identify our 'deepest desire'. But this stream does show itself sometimes in the conscious levels of our lives. Like a mountain stream it bubbles up in small springs and little fountains and trickles along the way. It seeps out of rock-faces and it feeds our mountain flowers.

These visible signs of the underground flow of our hearts could be seen as the desires we *know* we have. These trickles may show themselves as areas of our experience where we are consciously striving for some specific happiness or success or fulfilment; for example, the strong desire to get a good job (or to get a job at all), to find a partner, to travel the world, to have a child, and so on. Or they may be more obvious by their absence. We may notice dry patches of our lives, and empty spaces, and ask God, in prayer, to fill them and to take away the empty aching or the source of specific pain in ourselves, or in others.

But all the while the deep current flows on, holding our deepest desire, often unspoken and unrecognised. Without trying too hard to identify what, exactly, it really holds in its depths let us rather, for a while in prayer, simply be present to its existence, its power, and, above all, its benevolence . . .

And I discover, when I let my prayer become this deep flow that I can't even name or ever fully know, the amazing truth that God is *continuously* responding to it. Just as the parent of a much-loved, much-wanted child, is continuously aware of the child's fundamental needs and is continuously attending to these needs, even though the child itself is unaware of them, and indeed may express 'wants' that are not going to further their deepest needs and may even be damaging to them.

A strange reversal follows from this discovery. If I believe that God is continuously responding to my deepest desire, then it follows that by observing God's action in my life and his movement in my heart, I will be able to see more and more clearly what my deepest desires really are. Paradoxical though it may appear, I will become able to *hear* my prayers by listening to the *answers*, and not the other way round.

In a sense this is another manifestation of the Copernican revolution: my prayer, I find, is not really mine at all, but rather it is the expression of the movements of my deepest underground streams and currents that spring from God and are known and understood fully only by him. God's 'answers' are not brought about by my prayer at all, any more than the sun's movements are determined by the earth's. Rather, my prayer is the *response* to God's action in my life and his presence in my heart, just as the earth's existence is a response to the sun's.

In the previous chapter we looked at ways of getting in touch with what this deep current of desire is really about, in our personal experience.

We now go on to consider two areas of choice that we face, with regard to these deep currents:

- The choice about how we *respond* to our desires.
- The choice about *which* desires we will choose to follow.

What we discover about the way we are making these choices can reveal a great deal to us about how God is indeed answering our prayers through what he is doing in our lives, even though it doesn't always look like it!

The way we *respond* to our desires can determine whether our desiring is, ultimately, diminishing or expanding us.

The decision about which desires we will *follow* reveals the conflicts inherent in our desiring, and the way that conflict gets resolved according to our own choices.

A word about our feelings ...

Our feelings are the conscious signs to us of our desires. They are the first pointers to what our hearts are most deeply desiring or most deeply fearing, but they are also, according to the psychologists, the source of our *energy*. If you doubt this, remember how things were with you when you first fell in love, and how the energy that that state released in you made you think you could take on the whole world.

We don't have a choice about the feelings we experience – they are simply there. But we *do* have a choice about how we *focus* the energy they generate, and about whether we choose to nourish them or discourage them. We could say that the feelings themselves are in the 'Where' layer of our lives, our response to them lies within the scope of the 'How' layer, and the ultimate effect of our choices makes a difference to the 'Who' at our centre, which is where *transformation* happens.

The process of sifting out the deepest desire (and letting the others lessen in importance) could be seen as a process of *energy-focusing*. Just as a winter tree directs all its energies to the nurturing of its roots and its new, unseen, growth, and the summer tree focuses its energy on the production of leaf and flower and fruit, in order to reproduce itself, so our energy lines will vary through the stages of our lives, reflecting the movements of our deeply-felt desires. There is a natural cycle in energy-directing, that is mirrored in the cycles of our spiritual growth.

The most obvious detonation of positive energy that we can ever know is the Easter Resurrection energy that released, and continues to release, Life out of Death. The root and source of that explosion was surely Love. Are our desires perhaps ultimately rooted in love and in the desire for union with the God, who is Love? And are our deepest fears perhaps to do with the awareness of the possibility of alienation from that source of Love, and the eternal emptiness of an abyss of lovelessness?

You might like to return now to any powerful feelings you have experienced recently, and ask God to show you the *energy* they are generating, whether it is positive or negative, how you are directing it, and how you might be able to direct it more effectively.

Give or take: responding to our desires

If you look now at the picture of the tree you will notice that the nature of the desires expressed on the right hand side of the 'tree' is very different to the nature of the desires on the left.

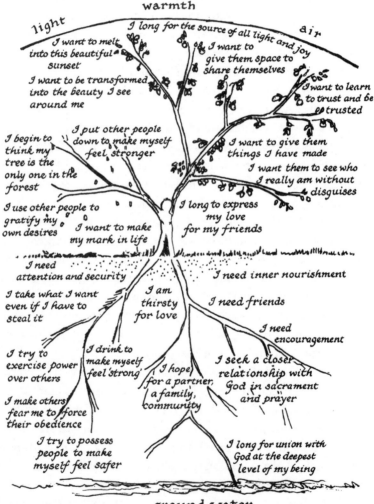

We have seen that our striving and desiring is always towards something beyond ourselves. But we have a choice about how we respond to that desire. One way of looking at this choice is to see our responses as either *taking* or *giving*. This might be a way of expressing the difference between the right and the left hand sides of the tree in the picture.

Taking desires boil down to a kind of inner consumerism. There is something that I desire, so I apply my energies to *possessing* the desired object. This might be something wholly legitimate, like a bar of chocolate or a book or a pair of shoes. Or it might be less tangible, like a job, or a qualification, that can't just be reached out for and taken. Or – and here the desire to possess becomes *illegitimate* – it might be a beloved person. Whatever it is, I have recognised a desire within myself and I am at least tempted to take steps to *draw that desired object into myself*. A familiar example of this kind of mindset is the phrase which we often hear and may well use ourselves: 'We had a weekend in Paris and *took in* the Eiffel Tower, Montmartre and a couple of museums.' It might be worth reflecting on what this kind of language really says about the way we view the world around us. It sounds harmless enough in itself, but is it about taking or giving, about consuming or responding?

Giving desires work the other way round. *They* do the drawing. Recall for a moment the feeling you experience when you listen to a piece of music that moves you deeply, or see a sunset or a star-filled sky, or gaze at a newborn child. Something tugs inside you and says: 'This is something utterly wonderful, and quite beyond yourself. You can never possess it, and you don't want to, because to possess it would be to spoil it.' Your response forces you to let the object of desire be itself, quite other, quite transcendent. There could never be enough space inside you to take in the object of your experience, even if you were to try. But the feeling remains one of desire.

There is a desire to experience this powerful feeling, this relationship, with what is drawing you towards itself. There is a desire to respond in some way, and often that response will come in the form of a leap of joy, experienced somewhere in the gut. You feel that you have indeed been expanded by the experience, but the object of your desire has not thereby been diminished. You also feel that the object of your desire has drawn something out of the centre of your own heart, yet you know that you have not been lessened, but, paradoxically, expanded inwardly by this drawing-out.

This difference has to do with what Ignatius meant by 'ordered' and 'disordered' desires. Ordered desires expand us without diminishing the 'other'. They draw us into a creative relationship with what lies beyond ourselves without tempting us to try to possess it. They represent a moving out of ourselves, a surrendering of something in our hearts to the power of the 'other'. They spur us into new steps along the inner journey. They lead towards transformation.

Disordered desires behave in the opposite way. They tempt us to suck things into ourselves, and result in the diminishment of the desired object. When I desire an orange, and take it into myself, the orange ceases to be an orange and becomes a part of me instead. This may be fine, when all I desire is a piece of fruit, but if my desire is focused on another human person, this kind of response to my desire becomes destructive. It destroys my relationship with the person, and ultimately, it destroys me too, as I pursue my desire obsessively and become more and more compulsed. More importantly, it can destroy the desired person, by suffocating them with my own feelings, unless they have the wisdom to withdraw from me to a safe distance.

The picture shows how this works in practice. We could take the spider as a model of desiring that is ultimately destructive, while the bee demonstrates a different, creative way of desiring and of fulfilling that desire. Can you identify any of your own desires and your responses to them with either the spider model or the bee model?

Give, or take...

Would I rather be a spider...

Whatever comes into my web,
(the force-field of my personality)
I shall consume.
It is taken into me,
as into a black hole,
and is destroyed.
I satisfy myself at the
expense of that which
I desire.

Or a bee?

I feel drawn towards
what gives me joy,
and I receive its pollen,
but I leave the flower
undiminished.
I am filled, and the
flower is pollinated.
We are both enriched
by the encounter.

Survival of the fittest: choosing which desires to follow

A change of scene now: not the forest any more, but the football field, and the start of the season, when every hopeful Eleven is looking longingly towards the FA Cup.

When I reflect on my desires, I can imagine myself at the start of the season. If I were asked to write a list of the things I want, the things I hope for, the things I dream of, there would probably be as many of them as there are hopeful starters in the League Tables. You might like to try this exercise, and see whether you can identify any of your teams!

How, out of all this chaos, is the deepest desire ever to come through and rule my heart? I seem to be faced with a disorderly mob of wants and wishes, and their negative counterparts, my fears and resistances, and when I stop to look at them I even find that they are in conflict with each other.

A few examples:

- I want to take that new job, but I don't want to move house.
- I want to lose weight but I want to eat my favourite food.
- I want to speak up about that injustice at work, but I want to retain the good opinion of my colleagues.
- I want to belong to the Church but I feel obliged to object to some of the ways it does things.

The list of potential conflicts is endless, and yet the way in which they get sifted, in a kind of evolutionary process, is as clear and straightforward as the way teams either get eliminated from the championships or go forward to the next round.

>   *It happens in every choice we make!*

Like computers, our choosing seems to work on a binary system. We may feel that a choice is full of compromise, but if we examine it critically we will invariably find that we always choose the preferred course between two (or more) options.

A radical way of expressing this is to assert that

>   *'No-one ever does what they don't choose to do.'*

This sounds preposterous, on the surface, and indeed, the choice may well be between 'the lesser of the evils', but I have found this statement to be true in my everyday choices, and even in a situation where there appears to be no choice (for example under threat of violence), it still holds: 'I desire to stay alive more than I desire to express my opposition.' Some people have made the opposite choice in such circumstances, of course, and become martyrs for their principles or convictions.

It's easy to see how this logic operates in the unimportant matters. If I want to lose weight badly enough, I will give up some of my favourite fattening foods. Then the weight loss desire wins the match and goes on to the next round. There it may meet a stronger opponent; for example: 'Do I want to keep on losing weight, even if that means dropping all the business lunches?' And so on.

It's less easy to see it in the bigger issues. Consider this dilemma

>   *'I can't come to visit you because I can't drive.'*

The two 'teams' playing here are:

>   *My desire to visit you* (a positive feeling) v. *My fear of driving* (a negative feeling).

The choice is mine. If I want to visit you badly enough, I will overcome my fear of driving. And if I do, my fear of driving will be weakened, and next time my positive choices for mobility will have a better chance of winning! The 'survivor' will always be the stronger desire.

One thing is worth noticing in all of this: *the choice is ours*. It isn't anyone else's fault if I don't choose what I want. My own heart has the full freedom, and the responsibility, of the choice, even though I may think I am acting under coercion. This makes it sound disarmingly simple. In a way it is, but of course we all know that in practice it can be terribly hard, and sometimes impossible, in our fallen state, to make the choices we really want to make. But *knowing* our desires is at least a step along the way to choosing their fulfilment.

Everyday Choices

Meeting a friend for lunch. ✓   v. Finishing the job I was doing.

Staying longer in bed.   v. Getting up early for prayer. ✓

Replying to a letter at once.   Putting off saying something difficult. ✓

Watching television v.   v. Enjoying the silence. ✓

Phoning a friend. ✓ v.   Reading another chapter of my novel.

Keeping a low profile at work. ✓   v. Expressing my opposition to an injustice.

--- and what they may be showing me about my underlying desires---

I value friendship more than personal achievement.

I desire prayer and silence more than comfort and entertainment.

I fear confrontation more than I value directness and honesty.

Try looking back now on some of the choices (big and small) that you have made recently, and see for yourself which desire has won in each case, and whether you can discern a pattern in your choice-making. The picture on the previous page shows an example of how you might approach this.

And so, when I start to touch on the deeper desires (and fears) that underpin my surface wants and wishes and aversions, I start to narrow down the field. The rabble of village teams that started out at the beginning of the season moves closer to the quarter-final or even the semi-final. The contenders are fewer, but the conflict seems to be the more intense. There is Big Money involved now. The prize is my heart, and there are no holds barred. I begin to understand why my Deepest Desire is such a vital question on my inner journey. And I begin to appreciate the scale of the conflict.

God's Will and our desire: the key to transformation

Now seems to be a good point to pause and draw together the conclusions of all that we have been reflecting on in this and the previous chapter. When we do so, we may discover an amazing surprise . . . 'God's Will', that for years we had imagined as some secret coded message locked up somewhere in the Fort Knox of the Church's treasury, may suddenly become blindingly obvious to us!

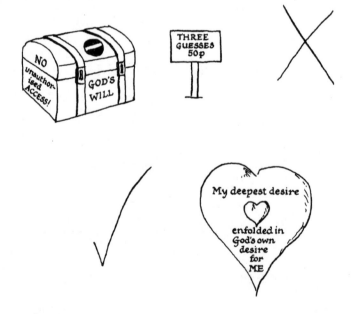

Let me explain how we come to this discovery:

- Among all my multitude of desires there are patterns evolving. It is possible to identify which of my desires run deep, which are forming my choices, and transforming me.
- In the struggle of my desires, I am choosing, minute by minute, that particular desire which is the stronger in me. Every time I choose in favour of my deeper desire, I reinforce it. It becomes dominant, until it meets an even stronger desire in me. In this way my lived experience gradually reveals to me my own deepest desires.
- I am directed towards God (fundamentally). It follows that my deepest desire is centred on becoming the person God created me to be (whatever that means for me in practice). However, as we saw in earlier chapters, even though I am fundamentally directed towards God, there will be movements and choices in me that are going in the opposite direction. What I choose in times of desolation (when I am temporarily turned away from God) will *not* be in line with my deepest desire. This is why we are warned not to let desolation change our course, and not to go back on choices we made when we were in consolation.
- Because my 'real' state is one of consolation and God-directedness, when I am really 'living true', my own deepest desire (to become the person God created me to be) is in complete harmony with 'God's Will' for me (that I might become the person he created me to be). 'God's Will', therefore, becomes not something remote and unknowable (that I will be punished for not carrying out!) but something as close to me as the deepest desire of my own heart, and something that he is only waiting and longing to reveal to me in every moment of my life and in every breath of my prayer.

    God's Will – his desire for me – and my own deepest desire
    (when I am really 'living true') are one and the same thing!

It follows that:

- Because God is continually carrying out his Will – his desire – for his creation (in spite of our obstructions!), I can be sure that he will always be doing, in my life, those things that further that deep desire.

- If I notice and attend to what God (through the positive movements, the 'good spirits' of my living) is *actually doing* in my life, this will show me what my deepest desire really is. It will also reveal 'God's Will' for me – and I don't need a map of the minefield after all!

Which all brings us back to the burning question with which this chapter began: *'Why don't you answer my prayers?'*

Now I can answer that question with a degree of painful honesty …

'You are answering my prayer, because you are continually nurturing the deepest desire of my heart (though I might not be doing so myself!), which is also your deepest desire for me, and your Will for me.

'If it doesn't feel like that, then let me re-examine, in prayer, those areas of my experience where I feel you are not answering my prayer, and see whether these areas are, truly, about my *deepest* desires, or rather about the lesser desires that would sap my energy and distract me from my search for you and for my own deepest truth.'

In the eye of the storm

All this discovery of the mortal combat going on in me between my mass of conflicting desires might, you would think, point towards a terrible final confrontation between my warring inner factions.

The good news is that quite the opposite appears to happen. In my own journeying, at least, I find that when I feel I am somehow touching on that which my heart most deeply desires (even though I may not be able to put a name to it) I experience a profound sense of peace. It may be fleeting and momentary, but it is truly there; it has the same quality as the sense of 'true north' that we explored in earlier chapters. Conversely, I can learn that when I experience such a sense of peace, I am close to touching on my deepest desire, and if I stop to reflect on what has brought me to this point, I may catch a glimpse of the nature of my deepest desire.

Why should this be? When all the desires (and fears) clamouring around my outer layers seem armed to the teeth and fighting for supremacy, causing turmoil in my heart, how can it be that when I penetrate the deepest levels of myself I find a singleness of desire and longing that is deeply at peace?

At the centre of myself,
where I am utterly vulnerable,
there is my deepest desire,
and my deepest desire is unarmed.

And this is not the peace of the victor over the vanquished! It is rather the peace that grows when all the apparently conflicting desires of my heart have been named, faced, accepted and integrated into who I really am. It is an *inclusive peace*, embracing all of me, not just the 'holy bits'.

Ironically, it was through a robbery that I began to sense this possibility of peace and why it is unarmed. One Christmas while we were away on holiday, our home was burgled. The intruders ransacked every cupboard, including those in a quiet room that we use for prayer and for days of retreat. Some weeks later, this experience returned to me in prayer, and I was surprised to find that in this room I felt no sense of invasion, even though I knew that hostile strangers had searched through its cupboards. Yet nothing of their spirit lingered in the room. Then my prayer itself seemed to reassure me that there *could* be no invasion, no threat in such a place, even if they had stripped the room, because what was in there – truly present – the spirit of the place – was *indestructible*, and therefore had no *need* of arms or defences.

But that prayer wasn't really about the prayer-room. It was about my own 'inner room', my own reality, my Who-centre, my true centre. It was about that heart of me where I feel utterly vulnerable because there are no defences there. And there are no defences there because none are needed. I have no need to defend my Who-centre, because, whatever is done to it, it is indestructible, just as God himself is indestructible.

Of course, most of the time we are only aware of the *vulnerability* we feel at our deepest centre, and we are much less conscious of its *indestructibility*. Yet at moments when our deepest desire is touched upon, and begins its transforming action within us, then we *know* peace – the peace that goes beyond all the struggle, and supersedes all the struggle – the peace that passes understanding.

In the eye of the storm is a centre of perfect peace, where our deepest desire is embraced as God's own desire for us.

When we experience these moments of peace we are experiencing a meeting-point with God which will reveal to us where and how transformation is beginning to happen within us. It is the space where we discover answers to the prayers we have not yet found the words to form, where we are forgiven for sins we have not yet recognised, and freed from prisons that we thought were pots of honey. That is where God is answering our prayers, continuously, because that is where HE IS, and where he engages our reality with his own.

8: WHY DON'T YOU ANSWER MY PRAYERS? – GOD'S WILL AND MY DESIRE
Suggestions for prayer and reflection

As they left Jericho a large crowd followed him.

Now there were two blind men sitting at the side of the road. When they heard that it was Jesus who was passing by, they shouted, 'Lord! Have pity on us, Son of David.' And the crowd scolded them and told them to keep quiet, but they only shouted more loudly, 'Lord! Have pity on us, Son of David.'

Jesus stopped, called them over and said, 'What do you want me to do for you?'

(Matthew 20:29-32)

Now let Jesus come to you, at the roadside of your journey.

He stops . . .

He calls to you . . .

'What do you want me to do for *you?*' . . .

How do you respond?

❧

Look back over your day. Did you experience any strong feelings, either positive or negative? What energy was generated by these feelings, and how do you think you directed that energy?

❧

Can you identify any areas of your experience that are fuelled by *giving desires*? Any that are dominated by *taking desires*? Where, in your experience, do you feel like a spider, and where do you feel like a bee? Take them into your prayer, and allow God to show you the difference between these two kinds of desiring and the effects they are having on your heart.

❦

During the course of the day, you will have faced countless choices. Remember just a few of them now. Which desires (or fears) were engaged in these choices, and which were the winners? Can you see any pattern evolving in your choosing of one course of action over another through the living of your day, or of your life in general?

❦

Remember some of the things you have been asking for in prayer recently. In what ways do you feel that these things connect to the deeper desires you are discovering in your heart? Now look back on the most obvious ways in which you feel God has been acting in your life recently. How do *these* ways connect to your deeper desires?

Have you experienced any moments of 'peace in the eye of the storm' recently. If so, thank God for them in your prayer, and remember them as anchor-points for future struggles.

❦

Centre yourself deeply into prayer. Allow yourself to be drawn ever more deeply into the heart of your own being, where God is indwelling. In that space, where you are most truly yourself, allow Christ to die on the cross. Allow him to descend into hell. Allow him to walk across the resurrection garden, his arms outstretched towards you. Invite him to show you, in his perfect way for *you*, that your deepest reality is as indestructible as his own Reality.

❦

As he began his journey as a pilgrim of God, Inigo, the former warrior, symbolically laid down his arms at the shrine of the Black Madonna in Montserrat. If you feel drawn to do so, offer your armour and defences to God in your prayer. As you do so, name each piece of armour that you feel you are using to protect your vulnerable heart – each disguise, each mask, each attitude that you use to shield yourself against the pain of being a living, feeling being. We all need these shields, to cope with the demands of life and of each other, but here, in your prayer, you are making this surrender to God alone, asking him to show you that your true centre, though utterly vulnerable, no longer has any need of them, because it is his own dwelling-place.

9. ADDICTED?

Recognising our attachments

We have spent quite some time with our desires – those two-edged swords that can either free us or enslave us! Without desire, there would be nothing to move us forward. Our energy is the product of our desires. If we had no desire for food, we would starve. If we had no desire to discover what lies beyond our range of vision, we would never take any steps at all, either with our feet or with our minds. You could even say that the existence of our desires is proof that there is a 'beyond' towards which we strive, and that creation does not end at the boundaries of our own hearts.

God created us with our desires. To deny our desires is to deny our whole human nature and the purpose of our being. So when does a desire become an 'addiction'? What is it that changes natural longings and strivings into destructive compulsions? I'm not a psychologist and I'm not going to attempt to answer these questions scientifically. I am only a pray-er who has observed the pull of compulsions in herself and who is learning to notice her inner compass, especially when it starts to wobble! Gradually, in prayer and over time, I am beginning to recognise when my 'addictions' are commandeering my energy, and when, by contrast, I am closer to my 'True North'.

The swing of the pendulum

I discovered the difference between 'True North' and the wobbles one night during a retreat. In the corridor close to my room, there was a big, old-fashioned grandfather clock. In the deep silence of the retreat house, which deepened even further at night, all you could hear in this corridor was the steady ticking of this clock. I often used to listen to its ticking as I imagined the long weight of the pendulum moving from side to side. It was this clock that taught me something of my own inner movements. My inner 'pendulum', I thought to myself, would be in perfect balance when it was hanging straight down, with no movement to either side. But this, I soon realised, was far from my normal state. More usually my pendulum was swinging out, to one side or to the other – often quite wildly. And I recognised these swings as the pull of my 'attachments'. There were *positive attachments* and *negative attachments*: things I *excessively* desired to have or to be, and things I excessively desired not to have, or to avoid. The picture shows how this might look. As long as the pendulum swings in moderation and balance, the clock stays true to its purpose and keeps good time. But if it were to swing excessively to either side it would lose all balance and reliability and become untrue to its purpose.

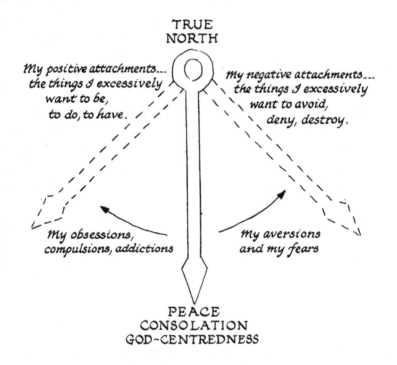

TRUE
NORTH

My positive attachments...
the things I excessively
want to be,
to do, to have.

My negative attachments...
the things I excessively
want to avoid,
deny, destroy.

My obsessions,
compulsions, addictions

My aversions
and my fears

PEACE
CONSOLATION
GOD~CENTREDNESS

Note the word *excessively*. One way in which we can tell that a natural desire is becoming a compulsion or an 'addiction' is when it starts to take us over, so that we begin to make our choices, not in inner freedom, but in the *desire to gain* what we want or in the *fear of losing* something or someone. For example, we have a natural desire to be safe, healthy and unharmed, but if this desire becomes excessive, so that we don't dare to go out of the house, then it has become compulsive. We have in fact become the slave of our own desire, and we start to live in a kind of dependency upon it.

Watering the weeds, or nourishing the crop?

Another way to look at our desires is to notice how we are focusing the energy they generate and whether this energy is fuelling our onward journey towards wholeness, in the life of God, or whether it is directed away from this life-giving journey. Suppose, for example, that I have an aversion (a negative attachment) to flying. This starts to become compulsive if I begin to arrange my life around it, by, for example, choosing not to visit friends overseas, or take a job involving travel. If this happens, I can find that I am spending more energy on finding ways of avoiding flying than I am on the positive, life-giving aspects of my life. In gardener's terms, I am 'watering the weeds' while neglecting the main crop! I am attending more to the things that are *life-denying* (my fears and aversions) than to the movements in me that are *life-giving*. And I have surrendered something of my inner freedom, and given myself over to a kind of slavery, dictated by my fear of flying.

Or the slave-maker could be a positive attachment. Perhaps I am excessively concerned with what people think of me and whether they like me. Almost everyone has a natural desire to be liked and accepted. It becomes dominant and destructive, however, if it leads me to be insincere in the way I deal with people, in order to win their friendship. Eventually the insincerity I feel within myself will pull my pendulum out of balance.

A person who can teach us much about what imbalance our attachments cause in our hearts is Pontius Pilate. Imagine yourself at Jesus' trial. Pilate is torn all ways: he wants to remain popular with the Jewish people, but he doesn't want to fall foul of the Roman authorities and ruin his career. He wants to stay on good terms with his wife, who has warned him about her dream, and almost certainly he doesn't want to be associated with the violence against Jesus. His 'Who-centre' is fragmented and his various fears and desires are making his pendulum swing wildly backwards and forwards. As a result, his energy is unfocused and frenzied, and he makes the choice that is eternally life-denying.

By contrast, Jesus himself is to hang in perfect balance on the cross, like a compass needle eternally steadied on True North.

How does my pendulum feel today?
Where am I spending my energy?
Am I attending to my addictions and aversions?
Am I watering the weeds or nourishing the crop?
Do I sense the peace of True North at all?

Jesus hangs in perfect balance on the cross~
a compass needle eternally steadied on True North~
dependent only on God, and utterly dependent on God~
the only dependency that is life-giving~
my own pointer to Truth.

The day after my night with the grandfather clock, I came upon a large crucifix in the grounds of the retreat house. As I stood there gazing at it, just as I had stood listening to the clock, something fell into place inside me, and I knew that my deepest desire had been touched by that picture of perfect balance. This was the opposite of my own (and Pilate's) fragmentation. This was a pointer to Truth.

You might like to look again at the picture on page 142 and see whether you can identify any of your own positive or negative attachments and notice how far they are pulling you out of balance and restricting your inner freedom to choose your course in life without inordinate hope of gain or fear of loss. And then let the picture below lead you to reflect on the weeds and the crop growing in your heart's field, and how much attention you are giving to the one and the other.

Where is my attention focused?
Where am I spending my energy?

On my crop or on my weeds?
On what is life~giving,
or on what is life~denying?

The discomforts of being 'hooked'

Another step forward for me, in recognising my own addictedness to certain things, people or circumstances came in the form of a language lesson and a picture. See whether either, or both of them ring any bells in the depths of your own experience.

- *The language lesson*: the English word '*dependent*', comes from the Latin verb '*pendere*', meaning '*to hang*'. The German word for '*dependent*' is '*abhängig*', meaning, literally, '*hanging down from.*'
- *The picture*: Imagine yourself hanging from a hook in the ceiling. You are clinging on to the hook for dear life, terrified, lest it should fail to hold you and cause you to fall into the fearful depths below you. The picture shows how this might look.

Life~in~all~
its~fullness

By HOOK

Can you give a name
to the hook?

Does your happiness
depend on it?

Are you starting to
arrange your life
around it?

Do you want it to
be like that?

The hook holds us back.

The shepherd's crook lifts us out of the quicksands and draws us forward, on our own two feet.

or by CROOK?

Life~in~all~ its~fullness

Let's take a closer look at what it means to be 'hooked' like this:

- See how all your energy and attention is focused on the overriding need to hold onto the hook.
- See how the need to grip the hook is distorting you, twisting your hand and making you stiff and lop-sided.
- Feel, in your imagination, the effects of hanging like this: the exhaustion, the strain, the stiff arm, the painful hand, the tension in your neck muscles, and so on. Your body is trying to tell you that it isn't designed to hang on one arm like this!

Can you give any name(s) to the hook(s) in your life? You might be aware of some thing or person or relationship, ambition or circumstance in your life that you feel you couldn't possibly get by without. Then ask yourself (but gently and compassionately!) these questions:

- Does my happiness *depend* on . . . (the presence of another person, a particular event or circumstance or achievement) and is this need starting to dominate my consciousness and sap all my energy? Am I starting to arrange my life around it?
- If so, do I *want* it to be like this?

Again, it must be stressed that we are not talking here about the natural inter-dependencies on each other and on our earth, that make us human. A 'hook' dependency is something that pulls us out of balance, one way or the other, and that prevents us from making choices in inner freedom.

Have a look again at how it feels to be 'hooked'. Just as our bodies are clearly not designed to hang on one arm, and our muscles would tell us that soon enough, so too our feelings will tell us if we are suffering from some emotional or spiritual 'addiction'. We need only think of the turmoil and anxiety we feel when we are inordinately attached to someone or something – the fear at the possibility of loss, the determination to cling – all these feelings are warning signals issued by our 'spiritual muscles', to tell us that our Who-centre, our real self, is not designed for such dependency.

Yet it seems impossible to let go our grip, and to 'come off the hook'. It seems as though that will only happen when something or someone cuts us down or severs our wrist, or when the hook comes out of its anchor and literally lets us down, in betrayal or disappointment. And all of these possibilities are unthinkably painful, and our hearts close up against them. With all the characteristics of one in the grip of an addiction, we prefer to deny the problem rather than face the pain of the cure.

We might recall Jesus' warning: 'If your right hand causes you to sin (or to fall into a dependency that threatens your inner freedom), much better to cut it off than to freeze your whole being into an addicted state.'

Now let your imagination go further. Let it envisage the worst scenario. The hook loosens and gives way, or some unexpected turn of events slashes your wrist and severs your hold on the hook. Perhaps you can remember times in your life when this has happened to you – when something or someone you centred your need-love on has been taken from you, possibly in the trauma of redundancy or in the breakdown of a relationship. Feel yourself falling. Feel the ghastly drop from the ceiling to the floor. Feel the pain of your landing, the bruising and the broken feelings. But notice something else as well. Notice the solid floor underneath you, which, though hard and cold, is not a bottomless abyss after all. Try, in your imagination, to stand up on this solid ground. Notice your legs and feet, now able and free to walk again. See how it feels to put one foot in front of the other and walk forward. For the first time, you are *free. Free to walk on.* An impossible dream, as long as you were suspended from your hook in the ceiling. Let yourself feel the returning use of your legs. It is a hard-won and painful freedom, but it *is* freedom, and it signals *growth.*

Learning to walk

I was reminded of this pain of becoming free one day when I was standing in a queue in the Building Society. As I waited in the queue I was watching the man in front of me. He was holding his small toddler son in his arms, as he carried out his transaction. When the time came for him to sign the transaction slip, he had to put the little boy down. Until that moment the child had been resting peacefully in his father's arms, his head resting quietly on the broad accepting shoulder. But when he was put down and required to stand on his own feet for a few moments, he let out a wail of protest and held up his arms in a loud appeal for a return to the known and the trusted.

As I watched this little scene, I could see events of my own life re-enacted, in times when my steady certainties and assumed securities had been blown apart by the blasts of unwelcome surprises. Times when I had found myself standing on a hard floor. And what had happened to the comforting, supporting, sustaining arms that used to hold me? And yes, I have howled in protest and instinctively held up my arms to be taken back to safety.

I asked myself some questions that afternoon as I stood in the Building Society queue. I asked myself whether I really wanted to be a toddler all my life. And then I asked myself which way of being was the more secure – to be held safe, but dependent, or to stand alone, and take my chances in a world that might turn out to contain no certainties except my trust in the presence of God?

The man in front of me finished his transaction and picked up his little boy again, and a contented silence was restored. He carried his son out into the market place. But I knew that *I* would have to walk, and that, in my heart of hearts, I *wanted* to walk, even through the pain of loss of my familiar comforts and securities.

What price *your* love? – A dialogue with the devil

As a test of whether you have any addictions, try pondering this little story from the Book of Job. The original text is in *Job 1:6-22*. I have adapted it! Insert your own name, at the appropriate points, and imagine the dialogue is about *you*.

One day, the devil was having a chat with God.

'Where have you been?' God asked him.

'Round the earth,' he replied, a touch defensively, 'roaming about!'

'Did you come across my friend (insert your name) in your travels?' God enquired. 'She's such a friend. She talks to me every day, and she's really trying to be the person I created her to be. You must have noticed her. I'm quite proud of her!'

'Oh, yes, I noticed *her* right enough,' the devil replied. 'But you know, God, she's not your friend *for nothing*, is she?'

'What's that supposed to mean?' God asked, bristling warily.

The devil shrugged, nonchalantly. 'Only what I said,' he remarked, provocatively. 'She's well looked after in her friendship with you. Look how you keep her safe and stable and in good health. Look at the good, supportive friends she has (name some of your friends). Look at the gifts you have given her (name some of your gifts). Look at how you have given her the gift of prayer, and how you smile your blessing upon all she thinks *she* is doing for you and your Kingdom. I call that a real fat-cat salary for her friendship with you!'

God mused to himself for a while. Well, yes, he was fond of .... and why *wouldn't* he bless her and encourage her, but the devil *did* have a point ...

The devil, always with an eye to the main chance, noticed this moment of hesitation, and moved in with the heavy artillery.

'Just what do you think would happen to her discipleship if all of that went – disappeared, just like that, overnight? Any bets she would soon see the dark side of the moon and start to wonder whether her inner journey wasn't just an illusion? Worse, I reckon she would turn on you, and all her love would turn to spite!'

God was silenced. The thought shocked him. But he *believed* in .... Maybe he believed in her more than she in him. At any rate, he was ready to risk his faith in her, right to the limits.

'All right,' he agreed. 'You can do anything you like to her outer layers. You can break her certainties apart and take away everything she values. But you may not touch her "Who-centre". *That* is sacred space. I give everything else of hers into your power.'

The devil was delighted. He shot off like a bat out of hell, before God could change his mind.

And poor . . . . , she was in for a hard time. One after another, all the things she valued were stripped away from her. It began with the things she had thought she could well do without, like (. . . . .). It really hurt, after all, letting them go, but it didn't destroy her. Then the screws tightened, and things she had always thought were permanent started to shake (. . . . .). It was then, when she thought she was in total desolation, that the devil struck the worst blows of all. She found herself bereft, overnight, of those things closest to her heart; things that seemed to be part of who she really, deeply, was. Night fell, inside and out. There seemed no reason to go on living. There was no reason to stay with a so-called life-giving God, whose consolations could run dry like that for no apparent reason.

She looked back to past times, when desolation had hit her. She remembered times when she had given up on God before and ploughed her own furrow instead. And then again she remembered times when she had stayed with the dream. It struck her that she had, after all, written her own script for living, and she was still free to write the script for the journey onwards – or for the journey backwards. Where did that freedom come from, she wondered idly? And why hadn't God shattered *that* as well, since he seemed to have it in for her?

So how does the story end? Does she stay with the darkness, or does she discover the free space, still intact and unharmed, in her 'Who-centre', where the next choice can still be freely made? Does the devil win the day, or is God's faith in his friend vindicated?

The *Good News* is that our journey with God is a journey into freedom. He invites us, over and over, to cut free from our inordinate attachments, and he does it, not with sticks, but with carrots, as we shall discover in the next chapter.

9: ADDICTED? – RECOGNISING OUR ATTACHMENTS
Suggestions for prayer and reflection

Jesus was setting out on a journey when a man ran up, knelt before him and put this question to him, 'Good master, what must I do to inherit eternal life?' Jesus said to him, 'Why do you call me good? No one is good but God alone. You know the commandments: You must not kill; you must not commit adultery; you must not steal; you must not bring false witness; you must not defraud; honour your father and mother.' And he said to him, 'Master, I have kept all these from my earliest days.'

Jesus looked steadily at him and loved him, and he said, 'There is one thing you lack. Go and sell everything you own and give the money to the poor, and you will have treasure in heaven; then come, follow me.'

But his face fell at these words and he went away sad, for he was a man of great wealth.

(Mark 10:17-27)

Try to imagine yourself as being present to this scene. Bring to your prayer your own longing for that 'extra something' that would change your believing from a flicker to a flame.

Ask the Lord to show you the blocks that are getting in the way in your relationship with him, and the hooks that are impeding your freedom to move forward with him. Ask him to show you your own personal 'riches' – the baggage that you are carrying that is overloading you and preventing your passage 'through the eye of the needle'.

Let him speak to your heart, and listen to the suggestions that arise in your prayer. As he speaks to you, notice especially the expression in his eyes ('Jesus looked straight at him, *with love*'), and hear his words: 'everything is possible *for God*.'

❀

Notice, prayerfully, how your heart's pendulum has been behaving today. Have there been any wild swings out to either side? Have there been any moments of perfect balance in True North? Does the pattern you notice indicate any larger pattern discernible in your life?

❀

Can you recall any time when you felt absolutely certain about a particular course of action, and went ahead with it in that inner certainty that it was right and true, knowing that, for once at least, you were following your truest instincts? Replay that incident now in prayer, and ask God to imprint in your heart the knowledge of how it really feels when your compass is reading True North, your pendulum is in balance and you are living – and acting – *true*.

�֍

Recall a decision you have made recently. Can you identify your reasons for deciding as you did: did you decide in the hope of gaining something, in the fear of losing something, or out of a state of inner freedom?

✗

In your imagination, take a walk around the 'field' of your life. Notice the blessings, the gifts and the fruitfulness and give thanks to God for all of that 'crop'. Now notice any 'weeds' that you know are there. Stand still and give them over to God, as you would leave a sick child with a doctor. Now turn back to the crop again, and thank God for it, asking him to help you to nourish it and share it.

✗

Can you identify any 'hooks' that are operating in your life? If so, name them, in your prayer, to God, and, perhaps, if you feel able to do so, to a trusted human friend. Simply to recognise and 'own' them is a significant step forwards towards being freed of them. If you can do this, you have passed beyond the stage of denial and have opened yourself up to healing.

✗

Have the circumstances of your life ever 'cut you down' from a hook, or some state of complacency or 'security' and left you bruised and frightened on a cold, hard, floor? Now, with hindsight, can you remember how you first began to recover from that shock and take your first tentative steps forward on your own two feet? Bring this memory into prayer, asking God to help you recognise the possibility of journeying on to 'Life-in-all-its-fullness' and to trust this possibility into an unknown future. (If you do this exercise, don't do violence to yourself! If the memory is still too painful, leave it in God's care until you feel more comfortable about reflecting on it.)

10. DON'T CLING TO ME

Pathways towards detachment

Is your 'God' a policeman, or a midwife? When you think of God, do you see a law enforcement officer, determined to keep you on the straight and narrow, or do you see Someone who knows you – and loves you, more than you know and love yourself and is attending your birth into Life-in-all-its fullness?

I hope that, having come this far in exploring your journey with God, you will have discovered something of God's midwifery skills and his urgent, insistent call to *freedom* in your life. Not the freedom that is the anarchy of lawlessness, but the freedom of the baby who leaves the closed, restricting spaces of the womb behind to enter the immensity of Life.

Of course, all our images of God are inadequate and some can be dangerously wrong. But I find the midwife picture one of the more helpful ones. Perhaps we can let it lead us on into our reflections on what 'detachment' might mean and how we can get closer to it.

For all of us, our first experience of the pain – and the promise – of detachment was the hour we left our mother's womb, and, screaming with shock, entered human life on earth. In what seemed like a brutal act, of cutting the umbilical cord and cutting us off from the pre-natal food supply, we were in fact set free to live our own lives.

So it began, and so it continues, in the ongoing call to let go of what is not (or is no longer) leading us closer to God, and to choose instead those ways that, for us personally, lead us closer to him and to the fulfilment of his Dream of us.

The meaning of 'detachment'

Ignatius urges us to seek the freedom of 'detachment', or 'indifference'.

Neither of these words carries weight in our own language or culture today. Both sound cold and uncaring, which is far from the spirit in which Ignatius meant them to be understood. A better word might be 'balance'.

In his *First Principle and Foundation*, Ignatius talks about 'making use of those things that help to bring us closer to God and leaving aside those things that don't'.

At first this notion seemed to me to be rather exploitative, as if the whole of creation were only there for us to select from it the bits that seem to serve our purpose. It didn't come to life for me until one day I was sitting in a quiet, sunny courtyard and found myself watching what was going on in the fuchsia bush beside the bench. It was late August, and the bees were constantly visiting the fuchsia. They would land, very gently, on those flowers that were fully open to receive them. They made no attempt to enter a closed flower, or to force the petals in any way. When they found an open flower, they crept into its depths, to extract the nectar. In doing so, of course, they also carried the pollen from flower to flower, bush to bush, thus ensuring further fruitfulness.

As I watched them, I realised that, although the bees were choosing the fuchsia flowers, and disregarding the other plants growing in the courtyard gardens, other insects were seeking *their* nourishment from other plants, like the creatures shown in the picture.

In choosing what was exactly right for them, they were not only receiving their own nourishment, but also playing an essential role in the fruitfulness of their environment. And in choosing one plant rather than another, they were in no way rejecting or denigrating the others. The secret of this harmonious, co-operative life seemed to lie in each creature being true to its own essential nature. Each gained what it needed for survival and growth from the source that was right for it, and it did so without harm either to itself or to the flowers. In fact, after each encounter, both insect and flower were left in a richer state than at the beginning: the insect had been nourished and the flower had been pollinated.

This picture seemed to me to be a very vivid illustration of what it might mean to 'make use of what leads to life' and to leave aside what, for each person as an individual, does not lead to life. It was a truly creative kind of 'detachment'. It led me personally a little closer to an understanding of what God might be calling us into, when he asks us to 'let go of' our attachments. The bees, I noticed, made no attempt to 'possess' the

What is life-giving for me
may not be so for you...

Out of all your lived experience,
Choose what leads towards life,
and growth, and God.
Choose the things that pollinate
your Godseed,
and leave the rest respectfully for others.

flowers, nor did the flowers attempt to trap and hold the bees. This was a free interchange, fulfilling perfectly the needs of the bees, the fuchsia, and the wider circle of creation around them.

The game of Monopoly gives us another good example of where excessive attachment can lead. If one player buys up all the hotels and utilities and amasses more and more 'wealth' and 'property', the game ceases to flow, because the other players have less and less, and eventually the whole thing seizes up. More sinisterly, we see similar patterns at work in the way we manage our economies and our international dealings.

We are led back to the first questions again: whose kingdom am I serving, my own or God's? It takes a lot of courage to recognise the truth that we are not in ourselves the fixed and permanent centre of things, but rather that we are beings *through whom life flows*. But when we do understand and acknowledge this, we discover that our emptiness will lead us more surely to our true purpose than our imagined fullness ever could, because life and grace, and God, will flow so much more fully and freely through empty hands.

Yet, instinctively, we step back from the brink of the flow. For most of us, most of the time, the main thrust of our energy is spent in building and maintaining our 'riverbank homes' – those things that make us feel secure and safe and important. Our jobs, our possessions, our ambitions. We construct a little world around ourselves that feels permanent and solid. Of course, we are human, as God made us, and we need to feel safe and solid. It's part of who we are. But only part. There is another dimension of our being – perhaps, we might say, the eternal reality of who we are, which is not at home on the riverbank but is longing for the flow of the river itself.

The journey with God does not deny our natural needs and desires, but it rearranges our priorities and nudges us constantly with the suggestion that he is calling us on, as surely as the ocean draws the rivers. Our attachments begin to look like riverbank constructions that tempt us to get out onto dry land and stay there, where it seems so comfortable, desirable and safe. But if we do, there will be no on-flowing for us, no on-growing, no progress towards the full freedom of the children of God.

Letting go of our riverbank dependencies will be painful and may even seem impossible, as we began to see in the last chapter. If you could ask a new-born baby how it would survive without the placental food, it would answer: 'Impossible!' But the midwife knows better. God is our midwife through all the trauma and the joy of our coming-to-birth in him –

and God is gentle . . .

Dealing with our addictions

An infallible cure for a headache is to drop a rock on your toe! I have tried this out, accidentally, in practice, and I know that it works. I may have been totally obsessed by my headache; it might have been flooding my entire consciousness, to the exclusion of anything and everything else; but as soon as I feel the effects of the rock on my foot, I will most surely loosen my obsessive attention to my headache.

The moral of all this is that it is part of our human nature to focus our attention on the matter that most powerfully engages our feelings, whether the feelings are of pain or of pleasure, of fear or of desire.

My attention
will be focused
where my feelings
are strongest...

The purpose of this chapter is to look at those things in our lives that are having the 'headache effect', in that they are taking over our consciousness and 'filling us up' in ways that may be preventing and blocking the flow of grace and life. We tend to think of addictions as serious chemical dependencies, on alcohol or drugs, for example. But an addiction is perhaps more helpfully defined as a programme of dependency, often on things that are harmless in themselves, or even completely 'good', which has become 'hard-wired' in us, to the extent that it is determining our whole way of behaving and relating to each other. At this point in our journey, therefore, we are asked to permit God to reveal our addictions to us, as one who comes to free us from captivity and begins by showing us where the knots are in the ropes that bind us.

A skating lesson

Another example may help. I have never managed to learn to ice-skate, but I have always admired those who can and thought how wonderful it must be to glide confidently across the rink to the rhythm of the music. If we let ourselves be there, in imagination, on the ice-rink, for a minute or two, we can perhaps discover something of the difference between addiction and freedom. At first we cling with both hands to the rail, gingerly edging our way round. The process is tedious and lumbering, and a million miles removed from the lightness and joy of movement going on in the middle of the rink where the real skaters are. It feels like an unbridgeable gulf between ourselves and them.

The learning process goes on. Perhaps we find ourselves able to let go of the rail with one hand and move painfully forwards, instead of sideways like a crab. Yet the dominant feeling is still one of fear: the fear of falling and the fear of making fools of ourselves. This is the feeling that is dominating our consciousness.

What might bring about the transformation from this fear-ridden rail-clinging to the joy of the ice-dance? I would suggest that the secret might lie in the music. Suppose that we were able to put aside our dominant experience of fear, and allow ourselves instead to be taken over by the music. Let's try it in our imagination. You have nothing to lose. You are on solid ground and you are not about to break a leg. Let the music take you over. Imagine it flowing through your ears all the way down to your feet. Let it take over your feet. See where it leads them. Watch as it leads them off into the middle of the ice. Don't just watch. Go with them! They are surer guides to your deepest desire than your fear-logged head! What, then, after all, *is* your deepest desire in this exercise? To stay with the safety of the rail, or to experience the joy of the dance? You can't have both. You have to choose!

All very well, you may say, but this has little to do with my lived experience. True, most of us are not likely to be much of a challenge to Torvill and Dean, but the same principles apply in our struggles against all the addictions, great and small, that impede our inner journey. The secret of transformation has to do with where our energy is really flowing. Is it staying with the fear, or tempted by the joy?

In more general terms: are we dwelling on the negative feelings and reactions in ourselves, or are we directing our energies towards the positive feelings? Do we more often ask ourselves: 'How do I *stop* doing this "bad"; thing?' or 'How can I find even more time and energy for this "good" thing?'

Two phrases that we might take to heart as warning signals are *'if only'* and *'what if'*. The 'if onlys' of our life give us an excuse for dwelling on the past, and on the unchangeable features of our circumstances: if only I'd worked harder at school, lived in a different country, had a different set of genes, had more tolerant parents . . . The 'what ifs' have the same negative effects for the future tense: 'I'd like to try, but what if . . . I should fail, my friends think I'm being silly, I lose my job, etc.' The thing about 'if onlys' and 'what ifs' is that we will never know in any case how things might have been, if . . . or how things will possibly work out if . . . So energy spent on them is quite definitely negative energy, and is not leading us closer to God, but is pulling us down more deeply into a spiral of desolation.

= PRESENT IMPERFECT

If only! *and* What if?
are false friends...

If only! *blights the present*
with regrets...

What if? *blights the future*
with fears...

Where is the vision that will lead me
past their ambush?

= FUTURE PERFECT

Sink or swim?

I discovered another picture of freedom one night while lying in a warm, deep bath. I had emptied one of the little plastic bottles of bath oil into the water, in the hope that its promise to be 'revitalising' would do something towards rousing me from the threat of lethargy and despondency that was lurking around the corner.

I watched, idly, as the bottle bobbed up and down on the water. Then I held it down and filled it up. I let it go, and watched it sink slowly down and settle on the bottom. I fetched it up again, emptied it, let it float. And so the play continued, filling and emptying, sinking and swimming.

My childish pastime made me realise that God sometimes does the same with me. I fill up, gradually, with all the things I desire and want to hold on to. The more I fill up, the deeper I sink, until eventually I lie like a lead balloon at the bottom of the bath, quite incapable of movement. Then something happens to 'tip me up and pour me out'. It is usually something unwelcome, that I resist with all my strength, but if it succeeds in draining me of all the 'attachment' feelings I have collected, then something new happens. The little bottle bobs up again, freed of its cargo of bath-water, like the one in the picture. Free, and light, floating, moving, responding to every wave along its journey. And all this is the gift of emptiness; only in my emptiness can I be sustained by the buoyancy of God's unfailing love and move on as he created me to move and to grow.

When the bottle of my life is full of my attachments,
and sinks to the bottom of my world,
then tip me up and empty me, Lord,
however loudly I protest,
because I want to float free
and move on with you, in you, to you ...

Using the stick, or scenting the carrot?

Like so much of what we have been discovering, with Ignatius, the truth is blindingly simple and obvious. The *deepest desire* leads most surely to God. Just as the pain of my foot was greater than the ache in my head, and I therefore diverted my energy from my headache to my injured foot, so too the magnetic power of the music and the desire to dance on the ice, will override my fear of falling and letting go.

God teaches us like the children we are. He uses carrots, not sticks. He *attracts* us through our own deepest desires, and not through threats of eternal punishment. He calls us to the joy of his presence by inviting us to discover, in our own deepest desires, his own overwhelming and passionate desire for *us*.

What does this tell us about how to deal with our addictions? Two possible strategies suggest themselves:

There is a way which we might call *the stick way* (or *the ascetic way*). This strategy says something like this:

- I am becoming aware that I have these particular dependencies, attachments, compulsions, crutches, idols (or whatever you may like to call them).
- I will spend all my energy in trying to destroy them.
- If my idols are like the Golden Calf of the Israelites, then I will attend to the matter of getting rid of my calf.
- *I* will *achieve* freedom in this way.

The second way might be called *the carrot way* (or *the way of deepest desire)*. This strategy says this:

- I am becoming aware that I have these particular dependencies, attachments, compulsions, crutches, idols, etc.
- I will *not* try to get rid of them by my own efforts.
- Instead I will use the energy I have (which is limited) to attend instead to those things in my experience where I feel 'right with God' or 'on solid ground' or 'living true'.
- These will become the music in my heart that tempts me into the dance and overrides the fear that keeps me clinging to the rails.

- I will not spend my energy trying to melt down my golden calf.
- Instead I will turn my attention to the holy mountain and my journey towards it, with all of God's surprises that it is revealing to me as I go.
- In this way *God* will *lead me* to freedom, without my even realising that it is happening.

We can notice significant differences between these two strategies:

- The first is *me*-centred, the second is *God*-centred.
- The first is laboured and heavy; the second is light and joy-filled.
- The first depends on sticks, the second on carrots.
- The first is centred on my *fears*, the second on my desires.
- The first is a burden, the second is an adventure.

As a practical exercise we might practise noticing those things in our immediate experience that are operating by the stick method, and those that are reflecting the way of the carrot. Which things, for example, are draining us of energy, and which are generating new energy in us? Are we in the habit of using the 'stick' on ourselves more than we follow the 'carrot'. Which of the individuals in the picture below do we identify with?

Trying to destroy my attachments?
Or walking towards the holy mountain?
Which way shall I invest my energy?

The promise of the garden

Jesus warned Mary Magdalene not to cling to him, when she met him in the Resurrection Garden.

Take time to reflect on that scene for a moment . . .

Mary thinks she really 'knows' Jesus, and she has staked her whole life on that knowledge and certainty. Small wonder that, out of the grief of Calvary, she clings with joy to what appears to be a return to *how things were*.

Jesus won't let her do this, because he is calling her forward to *how things shall be*. He knows that she can never be free to move on with him to this wholly new and unimaginable reality, as long as she clings to her dependency on the limited realities of what she has known so far. He loves her enough to cut her free from her riverbank certainties and draw her with him into the flow of Life.

In that brief, but timeless encounter, Mary, and we along with her, move forwards from the frightened person who seeks to take hold of what she so fears to lose, to the confident and empowered apostle, who leaves the garden to become the first channel for the flow of the Gospel itself. Mary, and we, are born into a whole new dimension of freedom, because Jesus has cut the cord of our former needs and dependencies and launched us into the promised fullness of Life-in-Him.

Stepping Stones

You might like to reflect on the following 'prayer-picture'. If it helps you, then use it to lead you into your own prayer. If not, then, like the bees in the bushes, leave it aside.

'Each breath a stepping stone to God.'

The words have made themselves at home in my heart. Prayer feels like that. I let the feeling paint its picture in my prayer today. I let myself walk into the picture, feel the swirl of the river and stand on the stepping stone. My whole prayer today wants to be just time standing there in your unseen presence, on the stepping stone.

The river is wide, so wide that I can't see the other shore, however hard I strain my eyes. The water is clear and wild, full of unseen currents, unexpected rapids, but calm shallows as well. I feel at home in the river, standing on my stepping stone, as on an island of truth.

Behind me on the riverbank is my little home, a stone-built cottage that keeps me warm and safe and keeps the world at bay. My cottage is my kingdom. The place to return to when the river runs too wild and too cold, or when predators stalk the shoreline.

There is something disconcerting in the view out over the water. What had seemed like a journey of adventure, when I set out on it, to cross the river to reach your Truth and your Kingdom on the other, invisible shore, is not all that it seemed. Because I can see only one stepping stone, and I'm standing on it. There is no way forward.

I can't do anything about my position. I'm standing here in the water on the one and only stone. All I can do is stand here, be here, be present to the present moment, and realise that there is no journey, because there is no way. Only a line of stones left behind me, but I don't want to go back. Truly, I don't want to go back.

For a moment I feel a wave of panic, but it recedes, and leaves me free to stand on my stone, breathing my air, feeling the spray of the water, listening to your heartbeat pulsing through creation. And waiting, just waiting, for you.

And then, when my heart is still, you are there beside me, silently placing the next stone in front of me and inviting me to take another step into the trackless waters. Another breath, another prayer, another stone. Just one more stone.

My breathing becomes steady, each breath a stepping stone to you. As time passes, I learn to recognise your ways, and to trust, when I stand in the middle of the fast-moving water, that you will always bring me one more stone – just one – and call me forward to one next step. I welcome your arrival, and smile my silent greeting to you.

I come to expect you. I know I can rely on you. I stand here on my stone, my little rocky island, and feel a ripple of anticipation as I turn towards the riverbank to greet you as you come. You are a little late today. You are still there on the riverbank, searching out the right stone for me today. And only now I see how you are doing it. You are taking the stones away, one by one, from my cottage on the riverbank. Already it is half demolished. You are dismantling my kingdom, bit by bit, to provide me with the way to discover yours.

10: DON'T CLING TO ME – PATHWAYS TOWARDS DETACHMENT
Suggestions for prayer and reflection

The parable of the weeds

Jesus put another parable before them. 'The kingdom of heaven may be compared to a man who sowed good seed in his field. While everybody was asleep his enemy came, sowed darnel all among the wheat, and made off. When the new wheat sprouted and ripened, the darnel appeared as well. The owner's servants went to him and said, "Sir, was it not good seed that you sowed in your field? If so, where does the darnel come from?" "Some enemy has done this," he answered. And the servants said, "Do you want us to go and weed it out?" But he said, "No, because when you weed out the darnel you might pull up the wheat with it. Let them both grow till the harvest; and at harvest time I shall say to the reapers: First collect the darnel and tie it in bundles to be burnt, then gather the wheat into my barn."'

(Matthew 13:24-30)

Let the Lord speak to you through this parable about the weeds and the good seed growing in the field of your own heart. You might feel drawn to ask him what to do about your own weeds (attachments) and listen to his guidance to *you*. Then ask him to show you the infinite value of the crop that is growing in you.

※

If you can imagine your life as a river between its riverbanks, in what ways do you feel tempted to build 'riverbank houses' for yourself? Where do you feel more comfortable – on the bank or in the flow? Can you see what draws you, and holds you, to the riverbank, and what attracts you onwards in the flow?

※

Is there something that you would really love to do in your life, but you don't yet have the courage to 'let go of the rails'? Bring your fear honestly before God in your prayer, and then let him direct your gaze towards your desire. Which has the stronger pull: your fear or your desire? Do you want it to stay the way it is or would you welcome change, and transformation? Lay your feelings before God, without disguises or excuses.

❀

Can you recall a time when you have felt 'tipped up and poured out'? Now, with hindsight, would you say that this experience was, in the longer term, deadening, or enlivening? Did it diminish or increase your inner freedom?

❀

Look critically at one of your 'attachments', that perhaps you very much wish you didn't have. How are you dealing with it now – using a stick or a carrot? Is your method effective? If not, what would you wish to do in order to change it? Bring your desire for change to God in your prayer and ask for the grace to re-focus your energy.

Have you ever in your life felt cut off from something or someone you thought was essential to your well-being? If so, recall in prayer the longing you felt to return to 'how things were'. Since that time your future has unfolded itself a little more. Do you still feel the same sense of loss and desperation, or has your experience moved you forward at all towards 'how things shall be'?

You might like to meditate on Mary Magdalene's meeting with Jesus in the Resurrection Garden (John 20:11-18). Show the Lord your tears and your grief, as she did. Hear the words *'Don't cling . . .'* Let Jesus touch your pain and infuse you with the power and the confidence of his liberating love for you, his unfailing faith in you.

11. RECOGNISING THE ENEMY; TRUSTING THE FRIEND

Before we look at the big questions around the promises and challenges of inner truth and inner freedom, I'd like to share a dream-story with you, that left me with what I think may be a useful picture of what can happen when we are 'hooked'.

In my dream I was travelling in a train. Before we had travelled far, the driver himself came to visit me, and showed me the map of our journey. I didn't know the places we would pass through – they didn't mean anything to me – they were all part of a still unknown future – but the driver traced the route on the map with his finger, smiled at me and commented: 'We will be travelling due North throughout the whole journey.'

We continued the journey and came to a station. It was a bewitchingly beautiful station, that had been a cottage but had been converted. Its walls were covered in vines, climbing plants and flowers, honeysuckle, clematis, fuchsia. Its little leaded windows were sunk deep in its solid white-washed sun-drenched walls. Along the platform, little tables were set out. Everything about the station invited the traveller to disembark, abandon the journey and settle in this beautiful place.

However, in my dream, I didn't disembark. I decided to stay with the journey. And after that decision the journey became noticeably less agreeable. I became aware that terrible things were happening, unseen, but guessed-at, on the train. Children were being killed; people were being ill-treated. Prisoners were being transported. I became uneasy and fearful, but the evil, whatever it was, remained invisible.

My fears became explicit when I noticed someone hanging on a hook from the buffers between two empty goods wagons. A cold shock-wave ran through me, as I realised how easily this person could be crushed between the wagons, or fall to his death on the rails below. But before I could do anything about it, a huge arm reached out from the top of one of the wagons, and a thick, grasping hand took hold of the person, hauled him off the hook, dropped him into the depths of the cavernous empty wagon and left him there with no way either of survival or escape. This 'evil arm' seemed to belong to some malignant presence that was part and parcel of the situation of the train, always travelling with it, wreaking havoc, but *not* (significantly, *not*) ultimately in control of it. The evil presence, though vicious and powerful, was not the driver of the train.

The strategy of enslavement

I awoke from my dream, that had almost (but not quite) turned into a nightmare. It was time to reflect. I knew that the dream had been important. Let me share those reflections, in the hope that you may find some resonance there with your own experience. This is what my dream taught me:

- The train, which you might see as our journey with God, was on an unswerving course due North ('True North'). The driver's reassurance was more powerful than any of the evil that was being perpetrated on board the train.
- The cottage, converted into a station, was so enticing that I *was* tempted to stay for ever in that 'place of consolation'. In fact, it had all the makings of an addiction – a hook. The word 'conversion' was significant. Even our deepest conversion experiences, because they are so beautiful, and so loaded with positive feelings, can become addictive, holding us bound to the signpost instead of journeying on to the destination.
- Evil is endemic in our world. It travels, invisible, insidious, on our journey, an ever-present threat. It brings about every imaginable destruction. But this invisible, intangible evil needs hands and feet, minds and hearts, to do its work. How does it enlist its troops?
- The 'evil arm' plucks the 'hooked' person down and drops him into the cavern of captivity. When I reflected on this moment in the dream-story, I realised a very simple, obvious truth:

Evil can get hold of me in the place where I am hooked. Like a fish on a line, I am helpless to escape its grasp as long as I am hanging on my hook. Wherever I am hooked, evil forces can (quite literally) do whatever they like with me. The next stage, after addiction, is enslavement! My hooks are the entry points in my life for the negative, destructive movements. And once enslaved, I can so easily be forcibly enlisted into the ranks of this false commander.

Evil can get
hold of me in
the place where
I am hooked.

And so Satan goes on his fishing trips, day by day, plucking us from our hooks, as we might pluck an apple off a tree, because in that position we are powerless to defend ourselves. So subtle is the process that we don't even see the risk; we don't even realise what is happening. And he doesn't take us off the hook to release us, but to enslave us, just as the fisherman takes his catch off the hook and flings it into the dark bowels of the boat, ready to be gutted and sold.

We needn't labour the point. Enough to realise that this macabre little tale illustrates, in a few short moments of dreaming, the *strategy* of the negative forces that are ranged against us, roaming our hearts, continually looking for ways of becoming embodied in our lives and the lives of our communities.

We can follow up this story, each in our own way. Once we are enslaved by our specific compulsions, we will find it increasingly easy to do wrong in order to keep ourselves 'supplied' with whatever it is we so need (which could be something intangible, like affirmation, popularity or power). Which of us has not, at some time, undermined a colleague for our own advancement, jeopardised a relationship to get our own way, risked our health and safety or that of others, to make a profit, lied or cheated to maintain our 'image'? Which of us has not allowed some addictive habit to become embodied in our character, distorting and polluting the whole way we live, feel and act, until, like a cancer, the habit runs out of control and starts to take us over?

Ignatius had a profound understanding of this strategy, and in his *Exercises*, he invites us to meditate on the 'two standards' – two flags raised by opposing commanders to rally their troops. One is the standard of evil, whose purpose is to *enslave* us so that we become puppets of evil ourselves. The other standard is that of Christ, whose purpose is to *free* us. Though the military imagery may not sit easily today, the underlying psychology of the picture rings deeply true. Both these commanders are on board the train of my dream: I have the choice, over and over, about which of them will drive the train of my life.

And the strategy of liberation?

On the face of it, it doesn't sound very inviting. It is about all those things that keep us hooked and about all the agony of 'coming off the hooks'. As we have noticed, in our own painful experience, getting unhooked can be devastating. It feels like losing so much of what we most value. Freedom is costly. We pay with the currency of our hearts. The difference, when we surrender to the liberator, is that we are asked to *choose* our own destiny, rather than being the puppet-slaves of our compulsions. In my dream this choice was reflected in the decision not to settle in the beautiful station, but to risk the onward journey. This was also a choice between a deep desire (to stay in the beautiful place), and an even deeper desire (to travel on). The choice I made was a reflection of my own deepest desiring.

At the moment of choosing, the options seemed unequal. The immediate fascination of the station-stop looked far more attractive than the rigours of the journey still to come. So why did I opt for the journey? Surely, because my deepest desire was to reach the longed-for destination (True North!), and this desire was stronger than the desire to stay in the place of consolation, and strong enough to help me through the barriers of difficulty along the way. This points, perhaps, to a thumb-nail sketch of the strategy of liberation. It seems to work something like this:

- I start to realise that everything I have – including my time, my talents, my feelings, my circumstances, and even those things I am 'hooked' to, are all gift.

- I don't have – and can't (by the nature of things) have any permanent 'hold' on anything, because I myself am only passing through the created world at this moment in time, and everything else is equally transient. To try to 'hold on' to things (or people) is to reverse the natural logic of creation, and set myself up, as it were, as creator myself.

- Because nothing is 'mine' in any real or permanent way, I have (ultimately) nothing to fear from apparent losses in my life, and (ultimately) nothing to gain from transient acquisitions or achievements – though of course it won't *feel* like this at the surface of myself. If I can begin to live from the free centre where these things are really true for me, I become free of the constant need to hold on to what I fear to lose, or to strive neurotically after what I obsessively hope to gain. All the energy that has been needed to maintain this 'holding on' and 'striving after' becomes freed for the thrilling challenge of becoming who I really am.

- Paradoxically, this doesn't diminish my delight in creation and all its gifts: quite the opposite. I find, when I stop seeing other things and other people primarily as contributors to my own well-being, and through the blinkers of how I can 'obtain' them or 'keep' them, or even 'get rid of' them, I find that my whole vision widens out and I begin to see these objects or these people *as they really are*: quite separate and 'other' from me, and pregnant with their own mystery. It's as if a distorting filter had been removed from the lenses of my vision. People are no longer defined for me by my own subjective desires, or fears, but by their own objective reality. I am free to enter into true relationship with them, and they with me. One thread in the tapestry of life has been redeemed.

The fictitious story below may help to illustrate this process.

Christine was the mother of a teenage son, Derek. As he came closer to the age when he would leave home, she became increasingly obsessed with keeping him close to her. Her great fear of 'losing' him stemmed from her fear of the loneliness that would invade her life, when he was no longer living at home. This fear was becoming her main motivator.

It followed that she began to see everything that Derek did or said in terms of this deep-seated fear. If he had a girlfriend, Christine feared to lose his love. If he showed interest in a course away from home, she feared to lose contact with him. If they argued, she feared to lose his good-will. She was 'hooked' to her need of her son.

To keep herself supplied with what she thought she needed, she began to use manipulative behaviour. She started to criticise his friends and invent stories against them. She started to 'lose' any mail that came to him from colleges away from home. She became 'ill' when he wanted to go away for the weekend. She gave in to his every whim, for fear of upsetting him. Their whole relationship became unbalanced.

It's not difficult to see the strategy of enslavement in this: first Christine becomes hooked to her need-love for Derek. She builds her life upon the false assumption that he is 'hers', and that she can 'hold on to' him. To keep herself supplied with this false need-love, she begins to do actual harm, interfering with his freedom and slandering his friends.

While she hangs on this 'hook', she is easy prey to the life-destroying, enslaving spirit that we might call Satan. He plucks her off, and drops her into the slavery wagon, where her whole life becomes a cage devoted to the retention of her hold on her son. Satan has won the day. The possibility of a real and free love between mother and son is destroyed . . . unless the liberating power can be allowed entry into the situation.

Now see how the strategy of freedom might reverse this process:

Derek makes up his mind to fly the nest, and takes up a study-place in a distant university. Christine is devastated. They have a massive row, and Derek leaves home. Christine's 'hook' has come out of the ceiling and she is lying, so to speak, in a crumpled heap on a cold, hard floor.

For the first time she comes face to face with the reality that her son is not hers to possess. This knowledge is bitterly painful, but it is potentially life-giving. It is a Calvary-moment. All her efforts to hold on to Derek, she now realises, were a futile waste of energy. *She lets go of them.*

After some weeks the first shock has subsided. She phones Derek and suggests a visit. Slightly reluctantly, he agrees and they fix a date for her to visit him in his new home. She begins to direct her energies into planning the visit. As she does so, she remembers moments from his childhood, and the happy memories give rise to a feeling of genuine gratitude in her for the times they have enjoyed. The store of memories becomes a source of renewed energy for her.

When the weekend of the visit arrives, she sees her son in a rather different light. Now he is an independent young man, with a group of interesting friends, and a vision of his own future. She is surprised to find how much he has changed!

In fact, of course, it is Christine who has changed – or, more correctly, her way of seeing her relationship with Derek has changed. Without the distorting filters of her need-love, she is free now to see him and relate to him as he really is, a separate and independent human being, full of his own mystery and a delight to be with.

Meanwhile, back home, now forced to face the lonely life she once dreaded, she is beginning to use her energies to discover new interests, in a lifestyle that is opening up more opportunities, to her now less clouded vision, than she had ever imagined possible.

And if we take this logic of enslavement and liberation into some of the political and social issues of our time, we will find much more dramatic examples of the insidious power of evil to infiltrate our relating and decision-making, and of the hard cost, but the rich reward, of surrendering to the way of freedom.

Watch out for the 'devil' in disguise!

Jesus warned us that other 'shepherds' would appear, who would, in truth, be wolves in sheep's clothing. Mostly we think of these 'false guides' as being external to ourselves, as indeed they may well be, in the form of manipulative leaders or those who turn the spreading of God's Word into a multi-million dollar enterprise in which they are the chief shareholders.

Ignatius, however, warns us of a different kind of threat from the 'false spirits'. We have already seen how they are present in the destructive inner movements that tend to lead us towards desolation, and, hence, away from

God. Even more dangerously, they can be operating in what *appears to be* consolation. Perhaps I can share an example:

Over a number of days my prayer had been centred on the events of Jesus' suffering and death, and the prayer had been very fruitful, showing me several aspects of my own life and journey that needed God's healing and my attention. I began to realise, however, that I was somehow resisting crossing the threshold from Friday to Sunday, and taking my prayer forward to the resurrection. Eventually I did move on, and tentatively tried to bring myself to the scene in the garden where Mary Magdalene meets the risen Lord. Imagine my reaction, therefore, after all this hesitation, when I 'saw' Jesus there in my prayer, holding up a hand to prevent my coming nearer, and saying, in quite a forbidding tone, 'Don't touch!' The prayer left me feeling desolated and distressed. I decided there and then that I wouldn't go back to that scene in prayer, and, indeed, that for a while at least I wouldn't pray at all! All this happened in the small hours of a tearful night. (This is a typical example of changing course during desolation and reneging on decisions taken during consolation!)

It happened that the next day I was going to spend the weekend with a friend with whom I am 'on the same wavelength'. Some time into the visit, I felt able to tell her about the 'Don't touch!' prayer, and how I felt about it. She listened quietly, then she spoke a wise word to me: 'Do you think that these effects were really from God?' she asked. At first I was so sure that it was Jesus I had encountered in my prayer and that those hard words 'Don't touch!' had been genuinely addressed to me and pointing to something I needed to look at. But as I reflected on my friend's words, I realised that the *after-effects* – desolation and distress, and a desire to abandon prayer – were actually the mark of a negative movement, or what Ignatius would call the 'false spirits'.

This was an example, I believe, of what Ignatius calls 'Satan appearing as an angel of light', or in more contemporary terms, of a negative movement in my heart infiltrating my prayer in a way that *seemed* to be wholly the positive experience of an encounter with God in prayer. In fact, the apparently harsh attitude of Jesus was really a manifestation of my own psyche, projecting my own anxieties onto Jesus in a way that was unhelpful to our relationship.

When this happens it isn't always easy to recognise it. One test is to look at the after-effects of the experience, and see whether they are leading you *towards* God or *away from* him. Another sound guideline is to share your experience and your reactions with a trusted friend or spiritual director, who will be able to reflect back to you the way the experience seems to have been working on you. This can be particularly helpful because, as you can see in my own example, when you are in the grip of this kind of negative movement, which appears to be so positive, you can be blind to the *effects* of your prayer and completely fail to register the obvious fact that these desolating feelings are *not* coming from God.

Let me just add, though, that it doesn't follow that because something comes up in prayer that feels hard and challenging, this means that it is not coming from God. It wasn't the apparently hard words in the prayer that betrayed the fact that it was not from God – it was the *effects* of the prayer on me. Suppose that the same words, in the same prayer, had left me feeling a desire to go back to God and ask him to take me deeper into their meaning for me. There might still have been tears, but they would have been tears of consolation, rather than the sobs of desolation. If these had been the after-effects, then discernment would have suggested that this prayer was indeed rooted in God. In this example, the effect of wanting to abandon prayer was the most telling clue to the non-divine origin of this inner movement. It was also a clear case for applying the 'Act Against It' rule!

People who are in a deep and loving relationship with God and have been practising discernment for years are often easy prey to this particular manifestation of negative movements. Therefore, beware!

When the fog lifts

Some years ago an elderly relative, Max, came to spend a few weeks' holiday with us. It was a wonderful autumn that year, and the trees were a joy to behold. Max seemed to enjoy his stay, but he had a strong attachment to his clothes! Which meant that, if they were to be laundered during his stay, we would have to sneak them away by night, and have them dried again by morning. This coping mechanism functioned well, but we hadn't thought of extending it to his spectacles.

Then, one particularly lovely clear morning he remarked: 'I do like it here, but is it always so foggy?'

It wasn't easy to convince him that the fog had its origins, not in the external world, but in the layer of grime on his spectacle lenses.

Is it foggy?

Or is it me?

The nature of the difficulty rings bells in my own experience – perhaps in yours too? I know that I can bring huge amounts of energy to bear on the task of convincing myself, and others, that the 'outside world' is where the problem is, and that the lenses of my own vision are immaculately clear!

It can be mortifying, when circumstances remove our spectacles and submit them to a humiliating cleansing. But the view thereafter is breathtaking!

11: RECOGNISING THE ENEMY; TRUSTING THE FRIEND
Suggestions for prayer and reflection

> 'I tell you most solemnly,
> I am the gate of the sheepfold.
> All others who have come
> are thieves and brigands;
> but the sheep took no notice of them.
> I am the gate.
> Anyone who enters through me will be safe:
> he will go freely in and out
> and be sure of finding pasture.

The thief comes
only to steal and kill and destroy.
I have come
so that they may have life
and have it to the full.
The good shepherd is the one who lays down his life for his sheep.
The hired man, since he is not the shepherd
and the sheep do not belong to him,
abandons the sheep and runs away
as soon as he sees a wolf coming,
and then the wolf attacks and scatters the sheep;
this is because he is only a hired man
and has no concern for the sheep.
I am the good shepherd;
I know my own
and my own know me.'

(John 10:7-14)

Centre yourself into stillness of heart, in whatever way is helpful to you, and try to recall a time or situation in your own life when you felt frightened and unguided in a dark, stormy night. (You may even be feeling like this right now!)

Read the passage slowly, as often as you feel drawn to do so.

In your prayer, listen, with all your being, for the call of the shepherd, coming to you through the storm. There is so much noise in the night, and your eyes are so blind in the dark. How will you know that the call you are hearing is the shepherd's call, and not some attacker pretending to be the shepherd?

Use your memory, to recall how the shepherd's voice has come to you in other situations in which you felt lost and threatened. Listen for those same tones now.

Out of all the clamour of the night, the shepherd's call rings clear and true to your heart: how do you feel now?

As you recall, or imagine, this situation, just ask yourself this one question: did *you* find the shepherd, or did the shepherd find *you*?

Can you name any personal 'hook' in your life that is making you easy prey to the negative movements in your heart? In your prayer, simply lay the facts before God and ask him to free you. In doing this you will also be laying the facts open to yourself, and this in itself will move you beyond the stage of denying the problem.

※

Try watching an evening's commercial television and reflect on one or two specific commercials. What signals are the advertisers giving us about our needs and desires? In what ways are they manipulating our anxieties and doubts about ourselves? Do you think that they are operating a strategy of enslavement or of liberation?

A way to check this out might be to ask the question: 'Am I being encouraged to claim something as "my own" and reap some advantage from that "possession", or am I being invited to let go of something and trust that in doing so I shall be expanded rather than diminished?'

You might like to take this kind of reflection a step further and apply similar questions to the way you see 'the Church' operating. Is it, in your experience, bribing you with rewards, threatening you with punishments, or truly accompanying you on your journey to the Truth? Is it facilitating your freedom, or colluding with your enslavement? If you feel uneasy with what you find, in such reflection, how might you begin to change it, bearing in mind that *we* are 'the Church'?

※

Can you identify any times or situations when you have come up against a 'false guide', either external to yourself, or inside your own heart? What makes you feel that this 'guide' was false? What tricks did this false guide use to try to seduce you into desolation and away from your True North?

※

Recall anything that you have done, or allowed to happen in the course of your life, of which you are ashamed. Don't judge yourself; just try to trace back to the roots of the wrong action, and identify the 'hook' that first began the downward spiral into this situation. If you feel you have since been freed of that hook, thank God for your liberation. If not, lay it before him in prayer and ask him to lead you closer to freedom.

❦

Children bring nothing into the world and they know their own power-lessness. If you have a chance to watch a young child's response to Christmas, try noticing whether he is still receptive to 'everything as gift', or whether he is already making demands and claims from a 'desire to pos-sess'. At what age does the child in your life seem to be passing from the first stage to the second? What might this tell us about Jesus' urging to 'become as little children'? Now reflect on your own response to seasons of gifting.

12. WHAT IS FREEDOM? WHAT IS TRUTH?

Pilate asked this second question of Jesus at the very point when Jesus himself had freely set aside his own freedom and allowed himself to be taken captive. Can you imagine the scene? The courtroom tension, the Passover, the excitement, the dawning knowledge in this man Pilate that there is something altogether different about the prisoner standing in front of him. Listen to his diversion tactics (it seems) as he asks the question 'What *is* truth?' in an effort to shift the focus of energy in the room away from himself and his deep unease about what he is getting into. Have you ever done that yourself, when a conversation got too close to the mark, by throwing out an apparent red herring to divert attention into some vague question that is safe precisely because it is so large and unanswerable?

But if we listen to the undercurrents in the courtroom, we may sense that these are not diversion tactics at all, but the first shaft of reality dawning in Pilate's heart, coming up spontaneously from the depths of his being and desperately seeking an answer, out of the space – the infinite space – between himself and this condemned man whose life hangs on his choice. Hear that moment when the clarity of his heart-need speaks above the clamour in his brain:

'What *is* truth?'

When I was first thinking about the kind of questions this book addresses, the question about freedom and truth seemed absolutely central. I had been confronted with Pilate's question myself, in an inescapable way, while praying the Passion, and living out in my own heart those Pilate-tensions. The question addressed to Jesus by Pilate seemed to come rolling down the staircase of the centuries, bouncing and echoing on every step, until it came to rest by my own feet and demanded to be picked up. My way forward with the Lord seemed to depend on my picking up this question and letting it hang there in the space that separates me from God.

Yet the more I have thought about it, the more preposterous it seems to me, even to suggest that these huge questions can in any sense be 'answered'. So all I can, or dare to do today, is to share with you one or two pointers that have brought some light for me, living, as I do, in the gap between God's truth and my falsehood, and between my captivity and the freedom into which I know God is drawing me.

When I hear Pilate's question re-echoing in my prayer, I know, increasingly, why it is so important. My old school had the Gospel words, interpreted by Chaucer, as its motto:

> *'And trouthe shal set thee free.'*

I lived with them for some years, emblazoned on my uniform, and resounding out of every end-of-term assembly when we sang the school song. Gradually they insinuated themselves into my heart, and sat there, like an egg waiting for fertilisation. It took over thirty years for that egg to come to ripeness, but when that finally happened, it took on a life of its own, as eggs do!

I knew all this when I began to think about these questions, and I knew too how central they are to any exploration of our inner landscape. But it was on a bleak November Sunday evening when something clicked into place, that helped me to take hold of the scale of the question, and it had to do with *the matter of the gap*. Let me explain . . .

Living in the gap

The words that triggered my understanding that evening could almost have been a cliché, had they not been spoken by someone who had obviously found them in the depths of his own experience.

God comes to us, he said:

- Not where we *should* have been, if we had made all the right choices in life
- Not where we *could* have been, if we had taken every opportunity that God has offered us

- Not where we *wish* we were, if we didn't have to be in the place where we find ourselves
- Not where we *think* we are, because our minds are out of true with our hearts, and
- Not where *other people* think we are, or think we ought to be, when they are attending to their own agendas.

I had heard this kind of wisdom often enough before. That God meets us *where we really are* is, after all, a commonplace of our journeying. We all know that with our *heads*, but that evening I suddenly grasped the truth of it with my *heart*, and that moment of truth brought me a new degree of freedom – just as Jesus had said it would!

And, really, it was all about the *gap*. The picture shows what I mean.

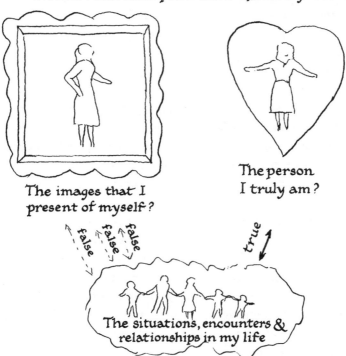

Which reference point am I operating from?

The images that I present of myself?

The person I truly am?

The situations, encounters & relationships in my life

I discovered that, when I look at myself, in any particular situation, or decision, or meeting point with others, I see two points – you might even call them *reference points*. One is the point where I really, truly *am*, before God. The other is the point from which I am in fact operating at that moment. This really only makes sense if we look at some examples.

I'm in the office. My manager calls me in for my annual appraisal. My next salary review depends on what is said in this meeting. My career prospects hang on it. So does my self-confidence. He asks me: 'How do you see the job developing over the next three years?' Look at two possible answers:

- 'I hope to be leading a team in three years, and taking on more responsibility.'
- 'I hope that in three years I'll be able to afford to get out of all this and do the things I really want to do with my life.'

The first reply comes from the reference point set by *where my manager thinks I am*. I am telling him what I think he wants to hear. It isn't true. The second reply comes from where I really am. It expresses my truth, in this context, but I almost certainly won't say it out loud.

Sometimes the untrue response goes beyond words into actions and life-changing decisions. Think for example, of the young man who commits himself to an unwanted marriage because his teenage girlfriend is pregnant. He is operating from where he thinks he ought to be, but he will live for years to come in the tensions of the gap between who he truly is and the untrue place in which his decision has been made.

The heart of the problem doesn't lie so much in how we actually reply or what we actually choose to do, but in the tension between where we really feel drawn to be, and where we are actually living out our days. The problem lies in this gap. But so does the solution! We begin to resolve this tension as soon as we acknowledge to ourselves, and to God, that it exists.

I'm sure you can multiply these examples, ad infinitum, from your own daily experience. Some seem almost too obvious to bother with – we all know these little dilemmas, and we learn to live with them. Others are potentially life-shattering. So what struck me so forcibly that evening about *the place where truth is*?

Well I think it was disarmingly simple, really. I suddenly realised that wherever God is in all my lived experience, he is in the place where I *really* am, and not at any of these other false reference points that so often dictate my choices and decisions. For me, this was a quite amazing break-through. *God-with-me*, wholly and lovingly present to me, at all those true places:

- The place where I recognise what I really prefer to do with my life.
- The place where I honestly acknowledge that what I am doing or deciding is at odds with my deepest desires.
- The place where I can say 'This is how I really feel', without the masks and defences that I wear to protect either myself from other people, or other people from the harsh stabs of my own true feelings.

Small wonder that I so often feel helpless, and hopeless, at the place from which I am trying to operate. It is not my true place. It is not the place where God is. And why isn't it the place where God is – for is not God in all things, and at all places? Again, the answer seems too simple to register, and yet profoundly true: God is not at our *false* reference points, because God is Truth, and he cannot be in falsehood. God is in the place *where we truly are*, because that is where he is offering us his healing, his forgiveness, his strengthening and his empowerment. There, and nowhere else, it seems to me, can we receive these gifts, and we reach our true place by becoming still before God and listening to his movements in our hearts.

A simple example illustrates the impossibility of meeting God other than at our true place, the place where we really are. I have a friend who is above averagely tall, who once confided in me that he wished God had made him a few inches shorter, because 'nothing quite fits him'. And another friend is below averagely short, and I have no doubt that he sometimes wishes he could 'add a cubit to his stature'. Yet if God were to speak to them *where they wish they were*, instead of *where they are*, I guess (physically speaking at least) they wouldn't hear him!

And much the same applies to our day-by-day actions and decisions. When we take them at the wrong place in our inner space – when we take them at a reference point that is not our Truth – then we won't enjoy the liberating power of *God-with-us* in those actions and decisions. Not because God is wilfully withholding himself from us, but because he is Truth, and our choices for falsehood, however excusable and understandable, can never be centred in him. They can never be True North, where our inner pendulum hangs straight. They will inevitably be affected by the movements that are pulling us 'out of true', out of balance.

Conversely, if we *do* manage to act out of our true reference point, we find that a whole new source of energy breaks open inside us. We experience *liberation*, freeing us to do the true thing, make the true choice, *from a place of power*, because there, and *only* there, our own desire, our own who–centre, is aligned with God's desire for *us*.

God, then, is with us where we really are, or where we are *real*, not at our false reference points. This may feel discouraging. After all, we do live much of our lives from these false reference points, but, though God, who is Truth, cannot be in falsehood, he can be, *and is* – so I firmly believe from my own experience – *in the gap*! He is in the gaps that open up between where we truly are and where we pretend to be, wish to be, or think we ought to be. He is not only the Truth, but also the *Way*. When we meet Jesus in prayer, and in our lived minutes, hours and days, we are meeting the One who bridges the gap between our falsehood and his Truth. Will we have the courage to walk across that bridge? The next chapter may help us to see how we might make the first step onto it, by bringing our own experience into focus with the Gospel experience, in our prayer.

Noticing the moment of truth

If you develop the habit of listening carefully to other peoples' stories, you soon begin to notice those times when what they are sharing with you touches their heart-truth. There will be a noticeable change in the energy level, indicated by their tone of voice or their body language generally. In some deep way, they 'come to life', they become energised, and you pick up the vibrations. Sometimes people can talk for hours – or, dare I say, live for years – without touching the 'truth button' in this sort of way.

But eventually something is said or felt, that causes them, inwardly, to change gear. It may bring them to tears, to laughter, to genuine self-disclosure in a conversation, or to a profound silence that you know marks holy ground. Perhaps a wall of stubborn resistance suddenly breaks down into a stream of tears that seem to flow from the person's deepest feelings. Or a controlled, courteous, 'correct' conversation flares out into a flame of anger, setting free a long-harboured festering resentment, for healing. This moment of truth, if it is grasped, can change the whole course of the person's response to the issue that is occupying them. It's as if some shell breaks open and a new way of being in the situation emerges, like a chick, with its own life and energy. But it takes courage to grasp the moment, and a sensitive companion can help enormously when such thresholds have to be crossed.

This makes it sound as if we live most of our lives entangled in a mesh of lies and falsehood. In a way, we do, and this is at the heart of our fallen-ness and our immense, immeasurable need of redemption. Not that we are *consciously* deceiving each other, or ourselves, in the big or small events and choices of our lives — it isn't that kind of deliberate sin. The web of false-hood holds us captive at a deeper level than consciousness. It slowly and insidiously programs us to operate from false reference points, until we almost feel at home and comfortable in doing so.

This way of operating generates all kinds of complications in our re-lationships — a web of hidden agendas and defensive postures that are designed to *conceal* our reality and our truth rather than to help us to disclose ourselves in trust and love. When we stop to reflect that every person we meet carries his or her own personal entanglement through life, we can begin to see the true proportions of the problem and to glimpse the extent of our need of healing. This consciousness of the deep-rooted consequences — both global and personal — of our fallen-ness can be devastating, but it is the hard rock foundation from which our journey to wholeness begins.

Yet, because we are so inwardly blinded, we feel *almost* comfortable in operating from false reference points. The word 'almost' is significant. The problem with operating out of falsehood is that it always leaves us with a twinge (or perhaps even a surge) of spiritual desolation. In some way, that we cannot articulate, our deepest desire — which has to do with being truly who we really are — is being frustrated, and our hearts are registering their protest through feelings of turmoil and discontent The way to healing begins when we learn to notice the moments of truth within ourselves, and to respond to them by *claiming the freedom* they hold for us.

An egg or an orange?

I remember one Christmas taking our young daughter to a Christingle service. The children were all given a lovely, ripe, succulent orange, decorated with the symbolic raisins and ribbon, and the candle as a sign of the Light of the World. It was a moving liturgy, and it wasn't until a week or so later, when the festivities were over and the orange was slowly withering, that it occurred to me how much truer a symbol of God's life in us, and ours in him, is the Easter egg than the Christmas orange. And now, as the memory floats back to me, I wonder whether the egg and the orange don't have something to tell us about Truth and Untruth.

Our untruths – our many false reference points – seem attractive and palatable and briefly satisfying. But as time passes they start to rot. They may carry us over the awkward moment, and briefly gain for us what we think we want. But they will not endure. They are like the house built on shifting sand, that will not, ultimately, withstand the storm. They are not a place where God can make his dwelling.

Best before: next week

My untruth
   is like an orange...
* It seems like hard
   currency to buy
   me love and
   acceptance
* It is palatable,
   while it lasts
* It soon shrivels and
   rots back into death

My truth
   is like a raw egg...
* It is fragile and
   vulnerable
* It is unpalatable and
   hard to handle
* It breaks open and
   brings new life
   into being

Best after: long incubation

Our truth, on the other hand, when we dare to name it and claim it, can feel like a raw egg – vulnerable, fragile and unpalatable, but (because it has been fertilised by God's Spirit in our hearts) it holds new life within it beyond anything we could hope for or imagine, and that new life has its own dynamic and carries its own new centre of energy. Paradoxically, our raw egg becomes a rock-solid foundation for a life rooted in our truth-centre.

Untruth holds, ultimately, only death and disintegration, but Truth carries Life, and when our shell cracks open in a moment of truth, something altogether *new* is set free.

Claiming the freedom

How might it feel, in practice, to observe our actions and reactions and reflect on whether they have their source in our truth, or in one of our many falsehoods?

We have already noticed how, when we are really 'living true', we feel as if we were in touch with a source of energy far beyond our own. We have recalled, for example, the surge of energy we experienced on falling in love, or on engaging in some project or activity that drew deeply on our innate gifts, or on becoming involved with something that moved us to active compassion or to a burst of creative expression.

To notice the difference between the limitations of our own energies and the power – and empowerment – that comes from the liberating energies of 'living true', compare, for example, the difference between cooking a routine meal for a picky, ungrateful child, and preparing a special birthday cake as a token of love for her. Or the difference between trawling round the supermarket for the week's groceries, and going to town to choose a gift for a loved one.

The difference hardly needs spelling out, because we all know it from our own experience:

- When I do something out of duty, I need to muster all my energies to cope with the effort required. When I have done it I feel drained. If I don't do it I feel guilty. I am acting from a false reference point; I am acting from *where I think I ought to be.*
- When I do something out of love, I barely notice the demand on my

energy – in fact the action seems to generate new energy inside me, that I didn't know was there, and the task becomes almost effortless. I am acting from my true centre, and the truth sets free my creative energy.

The difference seems to lead us back to that question of desire. When my deeper desires are engaged, I have more energy and I do what I do in a spirit of freedom. When my deeper desires are frustrated, I feel drained of energy and I do what I do in a spirit of reluctance.

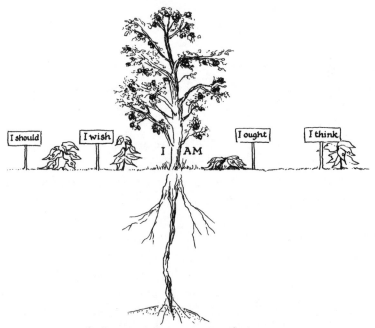

Only my truth is rooted in God

Those things in my life that spring from false reference points are like weeds that will fail to grow and bear fruit.

Those things that spring from my true centre connect to a source of energy and power beyond myself, which sets free my real potential.

So, as the picture shows, when it comes to my deepest desire of all – my tap root desire that is leading me to my truest centre – will I not find that my energy level rises exponentially, when that deepest desire is being nourished, but if it is being frustrated, the opposite will happen, and my vitality will be sapped and deadened? Like the Christingle orange, I will start to rot from the inside.

> *My deepest desire has to do with my sense of True North.*
> *When I feel that I am 'living true' (however briefly), I am touching into my deepest desire.*
> *When I am living true to my deepest desire I experience a new source of energy.*
> *This new energy frees me, and empowers me, to live out my inner vision.*
> *This liberating empowerment is the action of the Holy Spirit in my heart.*

How then, do I claim this freedom and this energy? Simply, I think, by attending, constantly to the inner compass that shows me when and where I am 'living true'. In other words, by practising discernment and nurturing the habit of living reflectively, so that each day I notice where God has been acting in my lived experience. These are the 'moments of truth', and if I ask God to release the energy that is latent within them, I will begin to live out, in my daily tasks and relationships, the dream he has for me.

Freedom *from* or freedom *for*

As early as the first chapter we noticed that there are two kinds of freedom:

- Freedom *from* an oppressive or destructive situation.
- Freedom *for* a radically transformed way of being.

The first kind of freedom is something that we may, and should strive for: for ourselves, to free us from the addictions and compulsions that we looked at in Chapters 9 and 10, but also for others, especially for those members of the human family who are less able to strive than we are, less strong, less empowered, less free.

The second kind of freedom lies at the heart of our desire for transformation. It is the journey to that centre of ourselves, which, as we have seen, is indestructible, and is the source of our truth and our energy because it is the dwelling place of God.

Sometimes the first kind of freedom can lead us on to the second. We struggle to become free of something that oppresses or diminishes us, and at first all our energy is focused on the desire for freedom *from*. But when that freedom has been won, either for ourselves or for others, the challenge to embrace the freedom *for* begins. We can see a vivid example of this in the struggle of the Eastern European countries in 1989 to free themselves from the oppression of state communism. Once the freedom was achieved, the much harder task of allowing that freedom to transform their societies began. Some responded to this new vocation. Others, like the Israelites freed from slavery in Egypt, wanted to turn back and revert to unfreedom with its apparently lower personal demands and lack of personal responsibility.

Perhaps a return visit to the circles of Where, How and Who may help. The picture shows how freedom *from* a destructive situation might be attempted, and sometimes achieved, by moving from one point on the Where circle to another, but that freedom *for* our eternal life in God is only found by moving into the Who-centre, carrying all our unfreedom with us, allowing ourselves and our hurting and captivity to be touched by God at that centre, and then moving out again, carrying the seeds of transformation back to the lived-out reality of our place in the 'Where'.

You might like to reflect on what you find in your recent experience of these two different aspects of the call to freedom. What destructive or oppressive situations are you aware of within your own circumstances? At work, in the church, in the family? Have you taken any action to free yourself from them? Has it been effective? Can you see oppressive situations that are holding other people captive in deadening circumstances? Can you do anything about it?

Now, by contrast, reflect on your personal experience of the second kind of freedom. Have you been aware of any 'moments of truth' in yourself, when you knew you were living in accordance with your deepest desire? How did you respond? Were you aware of the release of new energy in yourself as a result of touching your heart-truth? How did you direct that energy? How did you live out the freedom that flowed from that encounter with truth?

Freedom is its own reward

Once, while I was on retreat (and therefore more prayerful and attentive than usual!) I found myself reflecting on a particular situation in which I felt God was asking me to be more committed in co-operating with him in healing a damaged person. I wanted to say 'Yes', but I knew that my consent would be costly to me, and involve risk and vulnerability. Then, one morning, in prayer on a blustery hilltop, such as the one shown in the picture on the next page, up there among the furze bushes, I heard some inner voice saying:

'I won't love you any more than I already do, if you say "yes", or any less if you say "no".'

My immediate reaction to this was to feel aggrieved. Surely, I thought, my commitment to do 'God's Will' ought at least to bring me a few Brownie points on the salvation scale. But just as I was about to protest, the inner voice continued:

'Because to do so would be to violate your freedom.'

It was one of those moments when I knew, beyond doubt, that the 'truth button' had been activated. The *truth* that those words had expressed, had *freed* me of all the complications surrounding the choice, had left me free to choose:

> *Without fear of loss, and*
> *Without hope of gain.*

A meeting point
of my inner freedom
with God's unconditional love

Perhaps for the first time in my life, at any conscious level, I knew what it felt like to make a free choice. It also made me realise how very few of my choices in life are genuinely made in freedom. I, and I suspect most of my fellow human beings, almost invariably make choices and decisions that are at least in part influenced by our fear of losing something or our hopes of gaining something. If you doubt this, read the papers critically and see what is going on in Westminster, for example. How many parliamentary decisions are made free of the fear of losing votes or the hope of gaining influence? Which of our leaders or politicians are, in general, operating from a position of inner freedom? (There *are* some!) Now bring the focus back to your own world. Recall some of the choices you have made today, this week, this year. When you made them, was your inner compass reading True North, or was it swinging out to one side or another like the one in the picture?

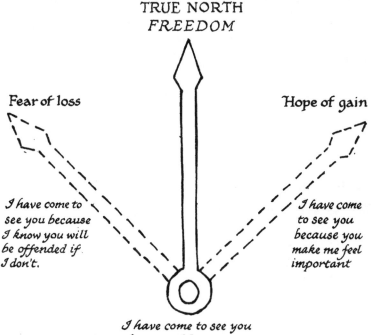

TRUE NORTH
FREEDOM

Fear of loss

Hope of gain

I have come to see you because I know you will be offended if I don't.

I have come to see you because you make me feel important

I have come to see you because I love you

God offers neither threats nor bribes.
He calls us into Freedom
and freedom flows from truth.

I made my choice that day. In that particular matter I chose to say 'Yes' but I chose freely, knowing that there was no 'reward' on offer, in the narrow sense. In that moment I learned how it felt to choose in freedom, out of my own deepest truth. And in that free choice, I noticed how all the complications of negotiating my 'terms' fell away, and how all the energy I had been using on those negotiations was released, to fuel the task to which I had committed myself.

It also released in me a sense of peace, which is almost impossible to describe, that made me realise that the joy of living and acting from my true centre (however intermittently!) is really and truly the peace that passes understanding, and the reality that satisfies my deepest desire, and that even the journey of my heart, home to God, is not about the hope of some future 'heaven' or the fear of some dark oblivion, but simply and solely the joy of each present moment lived fully, in the freedom of a child of God.

I learned there, up on the hill, what God had always known, that the freedom he was creating in my Who-centre was far more precious than any 'reward', and that my relationship with him, and with every human friend and neighbour, could only grow and bear fruit if it was rooted in that free centre of truth, of balance and of empowerment.

12: WHAT IS FREEDOM? WHAT IS TRUTH?
Suggestions for prayer and reflection

> *Jesus said: 'I am the Way, the Truth, and the Life.*
> *No-one can come to the Father except through me.*
> *If you know me, you know my Father too.'*

> (John 14:6)

Relax, and let yourself be drawn deeply into the silence of your own heart. Hear Jesus saying these words to you personally.

Ask him to open your eyes to see – first like a distant vision – the centre of your own *truth*, where he is indwelling.

Ask him, by the way of his cross, to make a *way* – a causeway – between your many untruths, and your deepest centre of truth in him.

Ask him to set free in you the energy and joy of his *life*, like a wellspring in your heart. With this courage kindled in you, begin to make the journey from where you feel you are, into your centre of truth, watching as the distance shortens and disappears.

❀

Look back over the past few days or weeks. Have you found yourself in any situation where you can see now, with hindsight, that you were not operating from your centre of truth, but from some false reference point? Take the situation into your prayer and try to re-enact it. Reflect on where you were operating from: for example, was it from where *someone else* expected you to be, from where you thought you *ought* to be, from where you *wish* you were? Now, in the silence, acknowledge your true reference point honestly, and without fear, to God. He tells us that he is the Truth. Try to become aware of his presence in *your* truth. However much you wish your feelings were not as they are, try to become aware that God is precisely *there*, in your true place, and that is where he loves and accepts you unconditionally.

❀

Now recall a situation when you have indeed acted out of your true centre. Re-live that situation in prayer. What was said, and done? How did you feel? How did things work out? Were you aware of any increased flow of energy or sense of empowerment as a result?

❀

Next time you are engaged in a significant conversation, make a deliberate effort to notice where the threads of truth are running. In particular, notice any moments when any of the participants (including yourself) touches on a real 'moment of truth'. What signs are there, to indicate the touching of the 'truth button' (tone of voice, body language, depth of self-disclosure)? Do you think the moment of truth is being acknowledged and affirmed by the other participants in the conversation? How might this moment become life-giving for the person concerned? For others?

❀

Which tasks that you have been doing today have drained you of energy, and which have appeared to re-charge your batteries? What have you done out of a sense of duty, and what have you done for love? How does this difference relate to your own deepest desires? Which tasks have been in harmony with your personal 'inner vision'?

❦

Is there anything in your circumstances or relationships that you wish to be free of? Let your desire for freedom be laid open in your prayer. What kind of freedom are you seeking: freedom *from* something that exists in your life, or freedom *for* something new, or both? Do you feel that God is responding to your desire? Tell him, in your prayer, exactly how you are feeling.

❦

Recall two or three major decisions that you have made in your life. As you look back on them, do you feel that you made your decision out of fear of losing something, in the hope of gaining something, or quite freely?

13. TO SEE YOU MORE CLEARLY . . .

It may surprise, and even dismay you to learn that so far, three quarters of the way through these explorations, we have been occupied almost entirely with those aspects of the inner journey on which Ignatius invites retreatants to reflect during the First Week of the *Spiritual Exercises*. All the huge questions – about the deepest desire, about addiction and detachment, about truth and freedom, about the realisation that God's overwhelming love for us is the very ground of our being, preceding and superseding our own broken-ness, about realising the scale of the mess we are in and the power and free availability of the redeeming love that alone can release us from it – all these questions centre on Ignatius' *First Principle and Foundation*, and on his guidelines for learning to discern the inner movements of our hearts by recognising consolation and desolation, and noticing when we are out of balance and when we are 'living true'.

In any building designed to last, the foundation is the most important feature. On our estate there is a house that is built on a site which turned out, when the first excavations were made, to be a former mine shaft. It doesn't take too much imagination to appreciate that more bricks and concrete went into the building of the foundation of that house than into its visible parts. The moral is obvious: the more unstable the ground, the deeper and firmer the foundation needs to be. For the great majority of us, the soil of our hearts, where God is making his dwelling-place, is extremely unstable. Which is why Ignatius, and we who learn from his wisdom, give so much attention to the foundations.

The prayer of Richard of Chichester, often associated with Ignatius, includes these three petitions:

'To see you more clearly,
To follow you more nearly,
To love you more dearly,
Day by day.'

This is a prayer that is so simple that it trips off the lips of children in primary school, yet so far-reaching that it can lead us to the very heart of God-with-us. The three petitions lead us, now, into the final chapters of our journey:

- To seek *to see the Lord more clearly*, by asking, in prayer, to become participants in the events and the teaching of his earthly life and ministry. This is the gift of the Second Week of the *Exercises*.
- To seek *to follow the Lord more nearly*, by asking, in prayer, to be alongside him in his Passion and death, and to share with him the joy of resurrection. These are the gifts of the Third and Fourth Weeks of the *Exercises*.
- To express our desire *to love the Lord more dearly*, by reflecting on what *we* can give *him*, in response to the immensity of *his* love for *us*. This is a gift of the contemplation with which the *Exercises* end.

And the prayer ends '*Day by day*', reminding us that the *Exercises* are not an end, but a beginning. The challenge of the journey is not to 'make the *Exercises*' but to live the truth and the freedom into which God draws us, day by day, as we seek to see, to follow, and to love.

Intimacy with God

We have spent quite a lot of time exploring what we most truly desire and discovering those things that are getting in the way of the fulfilment of that desire. We begin this chapter by asking ourselves: might it be true to express at least part of our deep desire something like this:

'I desire to know God better.'

We only need to reflect on what happens in human relationships, as the relationship grows and deepens. This happens when two people first of all feel drawn to each other, and then develop that feeling by revealing to each other something of who they most truly are. A relationship often begins with fairly generalised conversations where no risks are taken, as two people explore the 'facts' about each other – where they live, what they do for a living, where they spend their holidays, etc. This may grow into a rather deeper exploration, based on questions more like: 'Do you like your work? Do you wish you lived somewhere else? What makes you happy or sad?' And as the relationship grows and the two feel increasingly 'safe' and 'at home' with each other, more and more exposure can be risked. It becomes possible, for example, to say: 'I really admire you, but you make me feel inadequate, because . . .', or, 'I feel hurt because I don't understand why you said what you did.' It may even become possible to take the greatest risk of all, and say 'I love you.'

Suppose the same dynamic were to apply in our relationship with God. We may begin our friendship with God in the no-risk statements that we learned as children and we often express in our 'set' prayers. Let's take some familiar words from the Lord's Prayer and look at them in deepening ways:

'*Thy will be done.*'

We can chant these words almost like a mantra, rhyming conveniently with 'Thy kingdom come'. We may well have done that for years already, and we may well continue to do so, in all faith and love, for the remainder of our lives. Such prayer has its own power.

Or we may load the words with a little more personal meaning: 'I'm in a difficult position, Lord. I wonder what *your* will might be in all of this?'

Or our desire to know God more intimately might invite us to greater risk-taking: 'I'm finding this so very hard, Lord. It goes against the grain, but I really, deeply, want to do your will, and that desire is greater than my desire to do my own thing in this matter. Please help me.'

Or the greatest risk of all: 'Lord, I love you and that's the mainstream of my life. Let your will and mine become one.'

If you felt some resonance with the statement '*I desire to know God better*' then you are experiencing the call into deeper intimacy with him. If you respond to that call, he will draw you more deeply into friendship with him through your prayer and through everything in your lived experience. That friendship will develop by your revealing yourself more and more to him, and he to you, in a process of talking to *and listening to* each other, just as in human friendship.

Ignatius teaches us how to open ourselves up to this intimacy with God through Gospel-based meditation, through which we can, in our prayer, become participants in the life and ministry of Jesus and discover its reality for us where we are here and now.

Intimacy, whether with God or with another human being, challenges us to come closer, to take risks, to be open to change and transformation in a dynamic relationship which we cannot control. It engages us in:

- *Listening*, by opening our hearts to God. We learn to become inwardly still, and receptive to what God wants to show us.
- *Disclosing* – Revealing ourselves to God in prayer, *just as we are*.
- *Sharing* – Allowing the life of the Lord to become deeply connected to our own, by absorbing his Word, and by sharing in prayer in the events of his living, his dying and his rising.
- *Reflecting* – Deepening our experience of God by becoming more and more aware of the ways in which he meets us and greets us in our daily lives.
- *Giving* freely to others the gifts we have received ourselves; sharing God's love and spreading his Kingdom.

Meeting the Lord in imaginative prayer

The call to friendship with God invites us to allow our lives, and every-thing we most truly are, to become more and more closely linked to the life, death and resurrection of the Lord and to everything *he* truly is. This is what human friendship is about, too, but our friendship with God will take us deep into the hidden treasure within us, in a way that no human friendship can fully do. One way to allow this closer linking to happen is to enter imaginatively into scenes from the earthly life of Jesus, in what is called *imaginative meditation*.

Choose a passage that seems to speak to you in some way – a favourite Gospel scene, perhaps, or one of the healing miracles. If you don't know which passage to choose, just rest, relax and ask God to guide you; then wait to see whether any particular scene or event comes to mind. It is important to remember that God isn't waiting for you to chance upon the 'right' passage, in order to speak to you. He will speak to your heart in some way, whatever passage you choose. So be relaxed about it.

When you have chosen a passage, read it several times until it is familiar, and you feel 'at home' with it.

Now imagine that the event is happening here and now and that you are a participant in it, *active in the scene*. Don't worry if you don't find it easy to imagine it vividly. If you find it difficult to enter into the scene, imagine that you are trying to describe it to a child, making it as vivid as possible. And don't worry about getting the 'facts' right. You may well find that your 'scene' takes place, not in first century Palestine at all, but in the heart of Stoke-on-Trent, or the desert tracks of the Good Samaritan story turn into the hard shoulder of the M6!

Ask God for what you desire – perhaps to meet him more closely, or to feel his touch upon your life.

Fill out the scene as much as you can by, for example, becoming aware of who is there, of the surroundings, the sights, the smells, the tastes, the weather, the 'feel' of the place (peaceful or threatening). What role do you find yourself taking in the scene – for example, one of the disciples, a bystander, the person being healed? Listen, inwardly, to what God is showing you through your role in the scene. For example, he may be suggesting that you are standing on the edge of the scene and he deeply wants you to come closer, so that he can touch your life more powerfully. Or he may be asking you to take seriously a particular call to discipleship that he is suggesting.

Talk with the characters in the scene. Most especially talk to Jesus. Speak from your heart, simply and honestly. Tell him what you fear, what you hope for, what troubles you. React to him in your prayer as you would react to him if he walked into your room now in bodily form. Don't worry if your attention wanders. If you realise that this is happening, just bring yourself gently back to the scene, for as long as you feel drawn to stay with it.

There are two absolute rules:

Never moralise or judge yourself.
Always respond from your *heart* and not from your *head*.

This second rule isn't as easy as it sounds. We have been taught to *study* the Word of God, and of course it's right to do this. But there is a time, too, for recognising that our heads can never grasp the truths of God, and our purpose in prayer is not to come up with any kind of analysis or to write a sermon, but simply and solely to *respond*, from our innermost depths, to what God is sharing with us of himself.

So allow your feelings and your moods to have their say. If you have feelings of tenderness, or apprehension, or anger in the situation of your scene, this is telling you something about what is happening between you and God at that particular moment. Just as you take notice of how you are feeling and reacting in your human relationships, so too your feelings and reactions in your relationship with God are very significant, even if at times they may appear to be negative. We often learn more from our negative reactions than from the more comfortable ones, just as children learn more from their mistakes than from their perfect scripts.

You may ask – and many people do – how can I be sure that this is prayer, and not just a flight of fantasy?

To answer this question, you may find it helpful to apply these simple tests.

- Has my meeting with the Lord in this way *made any difference* to my way of being present in the world? Has it opened my eyes in any way, either to my own ways of acting and responding to others, or to the needs and vulnerability of other people around me?
- Is there a sense of consistency between what I feel I have been shown in this prayer and the way I feel the Lord is dealing with me in my life in other ways? If your prayer seems to send you off at a tangent and suggest a decision that is out of line with your personality or your commitments, then it is wise to be cautious. God's ways are usually (but not always!) gentle; and they are reliably consistent.
- Does the prayer leave me feeling basically at peace (even though it may have confronted me with hard challenges), and does the sense of peace continue as time goes on? When we follow our own daydreams, the sense of satisfaction is invariably short-lived. When the dreams are God's dreams for us, the peace is a lasting one, which will keep recurring and strengthening in our prayer.

Put more simply, we can apply the words of Jesus to our prayer: '*By their fruits you shall know them.'* Prayer that is given by God *always* bears good (though possibly painful) fruits in our lives. But be patient. Fruit can take time to grow and ripen.

You will see that a journey with God in imaginative prayer is a very personal one, unique to every seeker. However, it can be very helpful to share something of your prayer journey with another human being. This can help you to discern what God is saying to you in your prayer, because as you describe your prayer experience to another person, you will actually be describing it to yourself and you will often notice the threads of meaning then that you might not have noticed during the time of prayer itself. An attentive 'tuned-in' listener can reflect back to you what your feelings and responses seem to be and help you, as it were, to 'read the compass' in your heart that is pointing you towards God.

Focusing our inner lenses

It's probably true to say that all of us suffer, spiritually, from double vision. As we noticed in the previous chapter, we live out our lives' actions and decisions, for the most part, from false reference points. How often, during the past week, have you been conscious yourself of doing something that was truly rooted in your Who-centre, or of making a decision that was truly taken without fear of loss or hope of gain? How often were you 'in balance' and centred on True North? Sometimes the Truth seems light years away from the tangle of half-truths and compromises, postures and misleading attitudes in which we find ourselves operating.

However, as we also saw in the last chapter, God is not only our Truth, but also the *Way* to that Truth. The cross is the bridge across the gap between the places where we make our decisions and choose our actions, and the place where we truly *are*, before God. This bridge spans the expanse of chaos in which we often feel we are operating.

The Gospel is the story of the cross, and a map for our personal journey across its bridge, and imaginative meditation is one way of walking across that bridge. When we do so, we are opening our hearts to listen deeply to the Gospel events and stories and asking God to show us our own stories in the Gospel light, to make connections between what we are living vicariously in our prayer and how we are living in our incarnate reality.

Our prayer does one very simple, but potentially life-changing thing, if we will let it be done to us: it draws these two separate images together and focuses them into a single image, which is God's gift to us of a personal encounter with his Truth for us, in the circumstances in which we are actually living and relating to each other. The picture shows how this might look in practice.

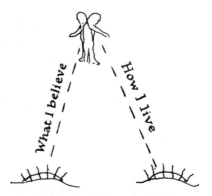

Prayer may reveal a bad case
of double vision...

and bring it back into a
radically new focus.

As this kind of prayer becomes a habit, we become more and more able to connect our lives with the life of the Lord, to find parallels between his teaching and our living. The picture of *God-with-us* gradually becomes more and more sharp, in our hearts, and as it does so, we are empowered to walk forward ever more confidently on our journey as our vision clarifies and deepens and becomes more searching. Clarity of vision brings sureness of step, and terrain that seemed to be wreathed in fog becomes negotiable.

At the same time, choices that are made from false reference points appear ever more obviously 'out of focus', and become disturbing to us. We have made our hearts over to God in prayer, and he is re-shaping us and conforming us more and more to his own image, his own desire for us, and to our own deepest desire for ourselves. When we ask for the grace to 'see him more clearly' he will answer our prayer, but he will also invite us to see *ourselves* more clearly, and this in itself will engender within us the desire to ask for the grace to conform our lives more closely with the Gospel values he is revealing to us.

Learning God's language

We believe we are the children of God. Children, so I understand, are born with the innate potential to form every known sound in every human language. Their first attempts at speech would be a medley of Babel-noise – and indeed, their 'speech' would stay like that, were it not for one thing. They all, even the least loved and cared-for among them, hear all around them the sounds of one particular human language – their 'native language'. They learn to speak intelligibly (at least to fellow native speakers), first by *listening*, and then by *copying* the sounds they hear. Quite simply, they learn the language of those to whom they are closest. A baby whose mother spends time holding her child and talking to it will become more articulate, more quickly, than one who is left neglected and alone for most of the day.

The same dynamic seems to apply in the way we learn to express the deepest desires and movements of our hearts. We will express ourselves in the language of the One to whom we are closest. Like a baby, our language will be formed by those we are close to. The further we draw away from God, the more garbled will be our heart's self-expression, like the image that is out of focus, until it reverts to the chaos of Babel. The closer we stay to God, the more surely our deeper desires will form around him and *his* desire for us, the more our way of being will be *conformed* to his.

At first our desires crowd around like a baby's first babbling, but slowly our 'words' are forming. We are writing the words of our own personal song of love. It begins in *listening*. It leads to *imitation*. It draws us, word by word, prayer by prayer into relationship with the Word, until all our words are superseded, and we are ready to be with him in a union of silence.

Stay close to the spring

When I think of my own need, and my desire, to stay close to God, I am reminded of a holiday visiting friends in the Czech Republic. We had spent a few days in Prague, where, amid blistering heat, the mains water supply had failed. No amount of hopeful lingering over the men down the holes outside in the street had brought any enlightenment as to when there might be water again, and our hostess struggled to keep things going as best she could by using the reserve bottles of water she had kept for watering her window-boxes. It was two days before matters returned to normal.

Soon afterwards we moved on to a remote village in the Bohemian mountains, whose only water supply was a communal spring. It was a joy to pick up the empty buckets and make my way on sandalled feet through the meadow down to the spring. The water bubbled up, full of a life of its own. I would place the bucket under its flow and stand back. No need for more than that. The water did the rest. It took a few minutes for the bucket to fill up. A few minutes of simply watching and waiting. It felt like prayer, simply bringing my empty bucket to the source of life and asking to be filled. It was suddenly obvious to me why human beings instinctively make their homes as close as possible to the water supply. And even as I was thinking these thoughts, my prayer seemed to form itself into the words:

> 'Stay close to the spring.'

Not reproachful or commanding words, but those of a cherished friend, imparting wisdom. Later I asked our host whether the spring ever ran dry. 'Only once in living memory,' he replied, 'and then very briefly.' And I remembered the day in Prague when the mains supply had failed and left us sweltering and waterless in the burning city heat. All the paraphernalia of mains systems and pipes and taps felt like the complications I place between me and God, and the more complications there are, the more distant I become from him, and the more unreliable are my inner resources.

I fell asleep that night with the words from my prayer murmuring through the rafters of the old farmstead: '*Stay close to the spring.*' That was several years ago, but the words became an icon for me, to which I often return when my heart is thirsty. You may find, if you explore the experience of imaginative prayer, that the encounters with the Lord that your prayer unfolds to you will stay with you for ever, a gallery of vivid memories, which will return to you again and again with ever deeper meanings for your life, until you feel you really do know Jesus as a friend. Yet there will always be mystery in your 'knowing'. He will always take you by surprise. As in any really significant human experience of intimacy, the relationship is not yours to control. Expect to be surprised, and let God do the rest!

To be close to the Lord in his human living, through prayer in this way, is to be close to the spring. It clears the obstructions and turns our man-made complications into God's own simplicity. It can be trusted, like the spring, and like the spring, it runs pure and free.

Finding God in all things

There is a marvellous bonus waiting for those who entrust themselves to God in intimate prayer. Just as you bring your 'all', your 'everyday' to God in prayer, and talk to him about how you really feel (which may well include expressing your anger and frustration with him from time to time – remember, that may be part of your Truth as well!), so, steadily, he will open up more and more of himself to you – or rather, he will increasingly open up your own inner vision, to notice him in everything around you, and to recognise his presence in every moment.

I personally have become convinced that there is nothing on earth that doesn't reveal some fragment of the Reality of its Maker, nor any moment that I live that doesn't hold God concealed within it. Sometimes this is obvious, as for example, in a beautiful sunset. Sometimes it remains hidden. Gerard Manley Hopkins, the Jesuit poet, calls it the 'inscape' of things – that inner mysterious reality that we might even call their 'who-centre', where God himself is indwelling. People have their inscapes too, as the next picture illustrates, and to be in an intimate relationship with someone is to be in touch with their inscape and allow them to be in touch with yours.

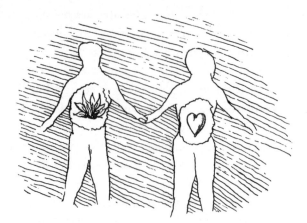

*You recognise my 'inscape' and I recognise
yours. We are in 'heart-to-heart' connection.
The God-with-you reaches out to
touch the God-with-me.
Emmanuel becomes incarnate in our relationship.*

We could use the picture of a net to help clarify this mystery. When I think of a net in this way I see a picture of the human family: every knot is a human heart, and every connecting thread is a relationship between those human hearts. And God is indwelling – if we allow him to be – in every heart-knot, and in every relationship-thread. To the extent that he is indwelling, the knot and its connections are sound, and the Holy Spirit flows through the links. To the extent that he is excluded, the net is weakened and torn.

Whenever I attend lovingly to the inscape of another person, I contribute to the strengthening of the net. Whenever I fail to respond to the heart-call of another, I weaken the net. It matters, how I respond – how I regard my neighbour-knots and how I look after the threads that connect us! It matters because this is the net that trawls through the oceans of the world in the hands of the 'fishers-of-men'. It is the net in which God is ingathering his children. Every knot in it has an inscape which is a fragment of God himself, and every connecting relationship is charged with his life and his love. I wish I could say that I always remain aware of this, when I am with a 'difficult' person, or in a problematic relationship! But the fact that I know what is possible, makes it all just that little bit more probable. And I am comforted to remember that the first disciples too had to spend much of their time mending nets!

*The threads of relationship make the net that holds
us in being and gathers us in to our homecoming.
God~with~us means each~with~the~other...
The two are indivisible.*

Beyond the joy

Friendship with the Lord, in the intimate relationship of prayer, is a gold-mine of joy that your explorations will never exhaust.

But friends die. If you have had the experience of walking alongside a dying loved one, you will know that there comes a point when words become meaningless. There is nothing left to say, or to do. If you allow the Lord to draw your life into his in prayer, he will, sooner or later invite you to walk with him to Calvary.

Like a very close human friend, only much more so, God will settle for nothing less than your absolute truth, the real essence of who you really are. He will die for the sake of that truth, and in some form or other he will ask you to join him in that dying and to trust him completely for the freedom and the life to which it is leading.

Friendship, if it connects heart to heart, is always costly. Intimacy with the Lord may cost you all you have. In the next chapter we will go on to face that cost and that risk, and reflect on what it might mean for the camel of our hearts to pass through the needle's eye of Calvary.

13: TO SEE YOU MORE CLEARLY – SEEKING INTIMACY WITH GOD
Suggestions for prayer and reflection

'I am the true vine, and my Father is the vinedresser.
Every branch in me that bears no fruit he cuts away,
and every branch that does bear fruit he prunes to make it bear even more.
You are pruned already, by means of the word that I have spoken to you.
Make your home in me, as I make mine in you.
As a branch cannot bear fruit all by itself, but must remain part of the vine,
neither can you unless you remain in me.
I am the vine, you are the branches.
Whoever remains in me, with me in him, bears fruit in plenty;
for cut off from me you can do nothing.
Anyone who does not remain in me is like a branch that has been thrown
away – he withers;
these branches are collected and thrown on the fire, and they are burnt.
If you remain in me and my words remain in you,
you may ask what you will and you shall get it.
It is to the glory of my Father that you should bear much fruit,
and then you will be my disciples.
As the Father has loved me, so I have loved you.
Remain in my love . . .
I shall not call you servants any more,
because a servant does not know his master's business;
I call you friends,
because I have made known to you everything I have learnt from my Father.
You did not choose me, no, I chose you;
and I commissioned you to go out and to bear fruit,
fruit that will last.'

(John 15:1-9, 15-16)

Take time to become inwardly still, and let these words of Jesus sink into your heart. Hear him speak them directly and personally to you.

You might like to reflect on how you feel, in relation to the vine that holds you in being, or in relation to the fruit your life is bearing. We are often as blind to our own fruiting as we are to our sinfulness. Perhaps ask God to open your eyes to notice the fruit on your branch of the vine, or to see which branches of your life seem barren and which are yielding a harvest.

How do you feel when Jesus calls you 'friend'? How do you respond to his invitation to stay close and remain in him?

※

Choose a favourite Gospel scene or story and try to imagine yourself a participant in it. As the events unfold, can you identify the two stories that are coming together? One is the Gospel story as it is given to us. The other may be a part of your own personal story, that in some way resonates with what you are meeting in the Gospel. Can you see these two pictures, side by side? Can you bring them together and let the Lord bring them into a new focus for you? You may feel that there is an unbridgeable gulf between them. If so, tell God so in your prayer, and show him how you are feeling. Or you may find that the Gospel story sheds a quite new light on this part of your own story. If so, let God lead you more deeply into what he is showing you in this way.

※

We are urged to 'stay close to the spring' – that is, close to our innermost centre where God dwells. What sacred spaces are there in your life where you feel 'close to the spring'? Which people lead you closer to the spring, and which, if any, tend to lead you further away from it? Look back over the past twenty-four hours: were there any special moments when you felt particularly close to the spring?

※

You might like to draw a picture of your own 'net', showing the 'knots' representing significant people, and the threads of relationship that connect you. Reflect prayerfully on the inner mystery of each person in your net, and each relationship, that we might call their 'inscapes'. Let the specialness and the uniqueness of each come into your awareness, and give thanks for it. Are you aware of any 'holes' in your net, or of any threads that are broken because a relationship is in trouble? Is there anything you can do to mend that bit of your net?

❁

Look back over today, and remember the moments when you have glimpsed the 'inscape' of something or someone – the moment when the hidden reality came alive for you in some way. Remember especially, with gratitude, those times when you have felt that you were relating to someone 'heart to heart'. Have those moments made any difference to how you feel about yourself? About the other person?

14. TO FOLLOW YOU MORE NEARLY . . .

Where is God in all of this?

How often have you asked yourself this question? How often have you been asked the same question by some other distressed soul? How often have we heard it asked out of the middle of some particularly inexplicable news item, reporting the heartrending suffering of the innocent?

And how often have we also heard the standard Christian answer: 'God is in the middle of the suffering.' And we have assented to that and thought: 'Yes, deep down we know that that is true.' But we have perhaps also wondered what it really means, how it begins to make sense of what we experience, how we could communicate that meaning to others, who so badly need to hear it. The question lingers, in spite of our own deeply held faith: 'Does this answer *really* convince us? Does it make sense of the pain we feel ourselves and the pain we see all around us?'

More than enough books have been written already on the problems of pain and suffering and God's place in it all. The purpose of this chapter is not to add any more to that particular pile of paper. Instead I would just like to invite you to follow one single line of experience which has helped me personally to find God in the *anguish*, as well as in the *joy* of my living, and which, I believe, lies somewhere close to the spirit of the Third Week of the *Spiritual Exercises*. This is the line of experience which, quite simply, draws a connection between our personal pain and the agony of Jesus in the last days of his earthly life, so that *his* pain becomes fused with *ours*, and ours is taken into his. This may sound like just another pious platitude. Only *you* can discover for yourself, whether it has real meaning for you, by letting yourself be drawn into the events of that Passover festival in Jerusalem . . .

Connecting to Calvary

In entering into the spirit of the Third Week, we are invited to pray the narrative of Jesus' last days on earth and to discover our own personal connectedness to the events of those days: the Last Supper, the betrayal, the arrest and trial, the torture, death and burial of *God-made-man*. The friendship and the intimacy with the living Lord, to which the *Second Week* invited us, now brings us up against that moment, which we may have experienced in our human relationships, when we are asked to be alongside a loved one who is suffering and dying. To be alongside someone at the very extreme of human experience like this, demands our whole truth, the real essence of who we really are. There is no more room for platitudes or ambivalence, for flattery, or any kind of half-truth.

When we are praying in the spirit of the *Third Week*, the question in the title is turned around. To answer the question: 'Where is God in our experience of suffering and dying?' God challenges us with his own question: 'Where are *you* in *mine*?'

In the *Third Week* prayer we are led to the discovery of those places where we are personally present to, and implicated in, the suffering and dying of the Lord. And in that discovery, he reveals, to our painfully opening eyes, the mystery of his own all-powerful presence in ours.

The cost of consecration

When we pray with the events of the Passion and death of the Lord, we are taking part in a personal Eucharist, in which he is drawing us into the very heart of his own consecration in order to consecrate *us* for his service. In our prayer we are consciously connecting the narrative of our own life to the narrative of the Gospel. Our purpose in bringing our personal narrative into connection with the Gospel narrative is to allow the power and the love of the Lord to become present in our lived experience.

In praying the Passion in this way, we come face to face with our own involvement in the events of that narrative. For example, we might find ourselves identifying with those who are hammering the nails into Jesus' hands, or betraying him for their own gain, or denying all knowledge of him, because of their fears. Or we may want to wash our hands of the whole thing, with Pilate, or run away and hide behind locked doors in the upper room. And in other scenes we may be filled with compassion and taken with the Lord as companions in his captivity and co-sufferers on the cross. Only in the depths of our own prayer will we discover what the Passion narrative is making present to our own personal lived experience and in what ways it is calling us on towards change and transformation. We are, quite simply, bringing it into the present tense of our today.

Recalling the circles of our WHERE, our HOW and our WHO from the first chapter, we could say that *Third Week* prayer brings the reality and the immediacy of God's suffering and death in his Son straight into the heart of our WHO centre, where it connects to everything we ARE. It allows us, with real truth, to say: 'Your suffering is mine, Lord. In my own small way, I have connected to it and felt it in the secret depths of my prayer. I offer you my heartfelt repentance for my part in causing it, and I offer you my heartfelt compassion in wanting to share it with you and make it a little more bearable.'

When we can do this, the transformation begins, and some glimmer of the mystery of redemption starts to penetrate our hearts. We discover that God, there at our centre, is responding to us in ways that we might express like this:

> '... *And your suffering is mine. Because you have opened yourself up to experience at least a small fragment of my suffering for you, so I shall fulfil my promise and draw you through this experience into the fulfilment of resurrection. The suffering and dying that you experience in your life may not appear to be alleviated in any way, but once your suffering has met mine, the deeper mystery is revealed.*'

And what is this 'deeper mystery'? Very simple, I think, yet infinitely powerful:

> *When our suffering is connected in prayer to God's, it becomes, like his, redemptive.*

This is the hidden power and mystery locked up in our suffering and our dying. The act of consecration, that our prayer has made possible, has released it and made it effective, to act upon the given-ness of our world and its narratives. It becomes redemptive, not just within the bounds of our own story, but for the story of the suffering of our fellow human beings, and perhaps especially for those we carry personally in our prayer.

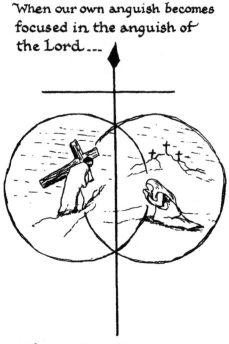

When our own anguish becomes
focused in the anguish of
the Lord ...

then redemptive power is
released, in ourselves,
and for the world.

Just as we saw in Chapter 12, the Truth that we encounter in the heart of our sharing of the Lord's Passion in our prayer, opens up a whole new freedom within us, which in turn becomes the source of an energy which is, potentially, the very energy of resurrection.

For breaking and sharing

For the Eucharist to be fulfilled, the consecrated elements must be broken and shared out in *communion*. Our consecration means nothing if it is kept to ourselves. Consecration is always *for* some purpose. It is not an end in itself. A church is consecrated for worship. A pilgrim is consecrated for his or her journey towards God. We are consecrated for God and for each other, not for ourselves alone.

Let's just think for a moment about what happens when, for example, we consecrate a church. It seems to me that we do two things:

- We declare our desire and intention that this particular place, this building, shall be a place of worship and a sacred space where God shall be at home.
- We then *use* that space for the purpose for which it has been consecrated, and in using it, we continue and fulfil the process of its sanctification.

It seems to me that God does the same thing for us when he consecrates us. He declares his desire and intention that we shall be consecrated to his truth and that our lives shall become a space where he can be at home. He then lives in our lives, fulfilling in them the purpose for which he has consecrated them.

And, like the Eucharistic bread, we are consecrated in order to be broken and given to others. Like the Eucharistic wine we are consecrated in order to be poured out for others. Consecration is always a *community* matter. It is an act of inclusiveness, expressing the all-inclusive love of God.

Consecration, understood in this way, is a vocation for *all* believers, and it has sacrifice at its heart. *We can't share in the consecration that was first enacted during the Last Supper, and is re-enacted in every Eucharist, unless we are willing to become part of the sacrifice.* Of course, it is easy to say, with our lips, that we are offering our suffering as part of Christ's sacrifice. And it is easy to believe it in our heads. It becomes a problem when we try to take hold of it in our hearts, because when it reaches our hearts it takes on a life of its own that rapidly passes beyond our conscious control.

What does this mean in practice?

How might our common human experience of pain connect to Jesus' experience on Calvary?

(Note that I say 'connect to', not 'compare with'. There is a huge difference. I can connect to the warmth of the sun, but I am not thereby comparing my own warmth to that of the sun! I can connect my kettle to the mains power supply, but I am not comparing its power to that of the national grid!)

Let's look at one or two ordinary human stories:

- Colin reported his workmate Frank to the DSS for moonlighting. He has often regretted it, because Frank was prosecuted, as a result, for benefit fraud, and his family split up. Colin didn't realise how badly he felt about it until he met himself in prayer in the garden of Gethsemane, planting the traitor's kiss on Jesus' cheek.
- Kate is trapped in the chronic pain of an immobilising handicap. In prayer she meets herself in the cell where the condemned man, Jesus, spends the night in chains, awaiting trial and execution. She follows him to the cross and shares, in a flow of tears, the stabs of agony as the nails are driven home. She offers her own pain to be joined with his.
- Julie is an appeaser. She will accept any compromise for the sake of avoiding confrontation. When there is trouble she tries to avoid getting involved, even if others are being hurt. She meets herself in Pilate. Her prayer breaks down in anguish as she finds herself washing her hands of all responsibility for the death of her Lord. She brings her shame to God, for healing and forgiveness.
- Mark was violently abused as a child and now, as an adult, he finds difficulty in controlling his own temper. In prayer he is appalled to find himself lashing out at Jesus with a whip, while some shadowy figure behind him seems to be forcing him to act like this. It is the moment when he comes face to face with the full realisation of the power his childhood pain still holds over him. It is the turning point towards healing and change.
- Jane's husband, Neil, was crippled in a car crash. Her young life changed overnight from one of unclouded happiness to a journey heavy with the burden of another person's needs and dependency. She often resents it. She finds herself praying, as Jesus did: 'Let this cup pass from me.' And as she makes the Calvary journey she meets herself in Simon of Cyrene, who, against his will, is forced to carry Jesus' cross. As she walks on, reluctantly, to Calvary, she comes to realise that the burden she is carrying in Neil is the very means by which God is drawing her into the unimaginable closeness of walking alongside the Lord.

- Richard is a doctor who nursed his own mother through the final struggle against cancer. He sat at her bedside, hour after hour, stroking her head and moistening her lips with a teaspoon of water. After the funeral he suppressed his grief and tried to pick up the threads of his life. Then, in prayer, he finds himself offering the dying Lord a teaspoon of cool water, and as he does so the grief breaks open in his heart. He watches, aghast, as the soldier pierces Jesus' side, feeling the Lord's pain in his own. And the teaspoon of water he had offered to Jesus as he was dying becomes a healing stream flowing from Jesus' broken body to bathe not just Richard's own grief, but the anguish of all those who will subsequently share their pain with him in years to come.

Piercing the darkness

These are simple stories of everyday human heartache. Stories of the pain we cause each other and the pain we recognise in each other. But they are also pointers towards the possibility of discovering healing, redeeming power in these very places that hurt us most.

When we risk the prayer of Calvary, we are taken to the threshold of a deep darkness. In Gethsemane, Jesus himself struggles 'even unto death' with that darkness that we ourselves experience to some extent in our own lives. In the heart of his struggle he reaches his own point of True North at which he can say 'Thy will be done'. When that happens, his pain becomes redemptive. It becomes a shaft of love that is sharp enough to pierce the darkness. The veil of the temple is rent in two and the glory of the Father is revealed.

... But it doesn't feel like that for us!

Perhaps I might share with you a picture that has stayed with me since childhood and grown in meaning through the years.

The Starmakers

One of my earliest childhood memories is of a night in winter when I came face to face with God while I was walking home from Brownies. If I close my eyes I can see the place again as vividly as it was for me then; I can return to the moment and experience the surge of joy that came coursing through me then.

I walked along the darkened side street from the church hall and had almost reached the junction with the brightly-lit main road. I can still see the red telephone kiosk on my left and the little sweet-shop on my right, with the waste land beyond it. And it was there, just short of the junction, that something urged me to look up.

The sky came down to meet me, and transfixed me there where I stood, for I don't know how many minutes. It seemed like eternity. Perhaps it was. All around me, in every direction, the black night sky was thick with brilliant stars, beckoning me, drawing me closer and closer, utterly eclipsing the street lights and any lights I had ever seen before. I could have stretched out my child's hands and plucked them down, like apples from a tree. The universe was ripe and straining with the load of the silvery harvest and I stood motionless in its enthralling grip.

As I recall my feelings at that moment I remember above all a deep sense of solitude in the face of all this splendour. I was alone in this overwhelmingly lovely eternal space, boundless in its emptiness, yet full to overflowing. Unimaginably vast and distant, yet close enough for me to reach out and touch it and hold it in my heart. I was quite alone, yet totally unafraid. The stars included space for me and there was nothing to fear.

The memory of that meeting returns to me often. I know now that it was no chance meeting, but one of the first of others that the years would yield and that would leave me ever more deeply enfolded in the arms of that loneliness and that splendour, in the arms of the starmaker.

Many years later I was taking my first steps into the prayer of the Passion, and struggling with the disturbing emotions my prayer was bringing into consciousness. There were two moments when my inner eyes came into contact with a darkness that was something much blacker than the darkness of the surrounding night, yet it was a blackness not really of threat but, ultimately, of promise, although there was plenty of threat surrounding that seed of promise.

One such moment was in the Garden of Gethsemane, when Jesus was led out by the guards and was just passing through a little gate at the edge of the garden. I suddenly panicked at the sight of his departing figure. I called out to him not to leave me there in the garden, not to leave me alone. He turned round, in response to my call. He looked straight into my eyes, and as I gazed at his face I saw, in his eyes, that deep dark into which he was allowing himself to be taken. 'Come with me,' he said, and I followed. The darkness had promise enclosed somewhere inside the threat.

The second moment was on Calvary. I couldn't let him die. I found all kinds of reasons to avoid praying through his death. I couldn't let go. But when the moment was finally reached, I met the deep dark again. I tried to stretch myself up to the full limits of my height, if only to reach just the soles of his feet, but the cross was too high. He was out of my reach. It seemed that at the same moment he tried to stretch his arms down to me, but they were nailed and rigid. I was out of his reach. It was perhaps the most terrible moment of the prayer, yet also a strangely consoling one, as our eyes met and I again felt him drawing me with him into that darkness that was utterly Beyond. We had met in the desolation of not being able to meet, and in that meeting I had clearly heard again that mysterious call into the deep dark.

My life moved on, but these timeless moments of prayer were to return to me again and again, and, as I noticed, this happened especially when I met someone who had in some personal way 'pierced the darkness' by embracing their own suffering with a kind of affirmation, as Jesus accepted the chalice of pain in Gethsemane. At such times I find myself standing beneath the stars again, seven or eight years old, but in my heart I carry all the pains and joys of the years between. And every star, every pinpoint of brilliant light, is where someone before me has pierced that darkness, gone through it with trust and with courage, without evasion or circumvention,

When someone dares
to pierce the darkness ...

... a new source of light is opened up
for those who still dwell in the night.

and broken through, however briefly, to the unimaginable brilliance beyond. And each, in piercing his or her own darkness, has opened up a new source of light, however small and distant, for those of us who still stand trembling in the night.

I am so grateful to those starmakers who have gone before, into and through their own inner darknesses. I can name many of them, personally known to me. Some who have gone out of sight for ever. Others who have touched the brilliance only fleetingly but still carry its fire inside them.

And I know that, in this great company, it might be possible to pass through the little gate of Gethsemane, in whatever forms it may present itself. I know that it will be possible, in some mysterious way, to let myself be drawn into the deep dark pools of Jesus' eyes on Calvary and discover the eternal radiance on the other side of darkness. For when every human heart has pierced the darkness, the darkness will be no more, and the Light of the World will be all in all.

An easy yoke?

Jesus tells us that his 'yoke is easy and his burden light'. Do you ever shudder when you read that promise, and wonder where you are going wrong, or how Jesus could have so misunderstood your situation? I certainly used to feel like that, and try to suppress the thought and refuse to let my doubts take root.

I think the promise only began to make sense for me when one day in imaginative prayer I found myself in the stable with the newborn Christ and his parents. I wanted to make myself useful, but, possibly understanding my inadequacies when it comes to practical talents, Joseph asked me to fetch water from the well to bathe the baby. My prayer took me along the dusty streets of Bethlehem until I reached the well, carrying the empty water jar awkwardly in my arms. I filled it up and tried to carry its now nearly unmanageable weight back in the same manner. Of course, the task was impossible. Then an Arab lady came up to me and gently balanced the water jar on my head. Then she drew my back and shoulders up straight until I was standing perfectly balanced. Finally she walked ahead of me, slowly, steadily, her whole body finely balanced. I followed her back to the stable, without spilling a single drop of water, and without breaking my back. I even had the peace and the space to enjoy the walk!

On another occasion, I was making my way, in rather a laboured way, up a fairly steep hill in Wales. As I plodded on, four teenage girls came towards me, riding down the hill on their bikes. Full tilt down the hill. As they passed me, every one of them greeted me with a wide, infectious smile, spreading their exuberance over me in an overflow of joy. One of them whooped as she rode by. God's own energy, it seemed to me, was propelling them, and gravity was moving them on, so effortlessly. They only needed to balance. The rest was pure joy.

When I translate this into the facts of my own lived experience, I really do discover that balance makes all the difference, and I think that right at the heart of my own balancing acts lies the kind of balance that Jesus teaches us in Gethsemane and on the cross: the balance between our own experience and the truth of God which it is making incarnate; the balance between our own efforts and the still centre of ourselves that we discover in prayer, where our true strength lies. When I feel now that my personal burdens are far from light, I try to regain that joy I have known when walking in balance. Of course it isn't a magic cure for my aches and pains, or for the sheer heartache of the Calvary journey, but it touches my truth, and it releases my innermost energies again.

An easy yoke?

If we learn to carry
it in balance!

Meeting the risen Lord

After Jesus' crucifixion, many of his friends encountered his living presence among them. These appearances seem to be characterised by two features in particular: first, the risen Jesus retained the marks of his agony, and invited his friends to 'get in touch with' the pain in him, as we have been doing in the earlier part of this chapter. Secondly, the friends frequently failed to recognise him, at least initially. You might like to take a favourite resurrection scene of your own into your prayer, and discover for yourself how the meeting feels for you.

Ignatius suggests that, although the Scriptures do not tell us so, Jesus would surely have shown himself to his own mother. Recently, during a retreat, my director suggested that I might spend time in prayer with that imagined scene. At first I was reluctant to do so. My protestant roots balked at something so non-scriptural. After lunch I set out to walk up the hill and see what the afternoon would bring, with Mary far from uppermost in my thoughts.

The wind was strengthening, but the afternoon was wonderful in its autumnity. The clouds were banking darkly in the west, but they didn't quite manage to obliterate the sun, that slanted down on the green-brown hillside with the glory of furze and the brilliance of berries.

Then, uninvited, Mary was there in my prayer. She was completely alone. She was broken and dumb with grief. She looked back over the thirty years of struggle and doubt, and promise and threat, of working to keep the dream alive, and grieving to watch it die. Thirty years. For what? Her own grief seemed to come out of her in a long silent howl: Love is dead . . .

I half expected to see the Lord appear to her, to comfort her and reassure her of his risen life, but nothing happened. Perhaps I never really believed that it would . . . ? She stood there, alone and broken, like an old hawthorn tree, bent against the wind, knowing that even its brief, berry-laden autumn would soon be swept into the mud, and lost.

Then there was a sudden change in Mary's mood. As if a new thought crossed her heart. Her face lifted, her eyes came to life again; she had noticed me, and touched into the pain she was reading in my eyes. She came over to me with a warm wave of compassion. For a moment her whole desire seemed to be to reach mothering hands into my lonely hurting. Something in me melted and surrendered to her love. Then just as she reached out her arms and held me to her heart, her gaze was captured by the miracle. I *knew* that she had met her Son, though he was invisible to me.

'Mary,' I whispered. 'Is he there?'

'My child,' she told me, her voice breathless with joy, 'he is standing behind you ... you are leaning on him.'

I didn't need to turn round. I could feel the power of his holding. But *she* had met him, in her reaching out to *me*. 'Go and do the same,' she told me, 'and you will meet him, risen and alive, standing always behind those who reach out to you in their need.'

I share this personal encounter with you because it seems, to me, to say something universal: if we seek the risen Lord, we will find him standing behind each of our brothers and sisters in their need, and he will become real for *us* at precisely the moment when *we* reach out to *them*.

Resurrection NOW!

The problem with eternity is that it doesn't fit onto our rulers. The infinite refuses to be organised into past and future tenses.

In the Fourth Week of the *Exercises*, we are invited to be present in prayer to the Resurrection, and, indeed, we may find such experiences in the scenes of Jesus' appearances to his friends. Like all the other Gospel events, these scenes will resonate with something deep in our personal lives, if we have ears to hear.

Yet right at the heart of resurrection is this mysterious sense of the present tense – *the ever-present tense* – that is not satisfied by our mere 'hope of the life to come'. In the Fourth Week we confront the paradox of the 'Now' and the 'Not Yet'.

I have my own definition of 'time', which helps me personally to take hold of this paradox.

> *Time, for me, is only the difference between God's dream and its fulfilling.*

I hope that, during our journeying together, I have convinced you of the reality of the Godseed in your heart, and directed your attention to the beauty of its growth in you. I feel sure that as soon as a human heart awakens to the life of its Godseed, resurrection begins, not just for that person alone, but for the whole human family.

Far from being passive spectators in the drama of redemption, we are co-operating participants, whose personal God-dream is an essential component of the fullness of resurrection.

Every time we touch upon our own True North, we touch the resurrection glory. Every time we feel the freedom that flows when we are 'living true', we are feeling the flow of eternity. Resurrection is a *now-moment*, a sacramental moment that at once both *points towards*, and *brings about* the fulfilling of God's dream. It is the working out, in time, of God's eternal Dream, and each of us is engaged in it, in every breath we take.

14: TO FOLLOW YOU MORE NEARLY ...
Suggestions for prayer and reflection

Then Jesus came with them to a small estate called Gethsemane; and he said to his disciples, 'Stay here while I go over there to pray.' He took Peter and the two sons of Zebedee with him. And sadness came over him, and great distress. Then he said to them, 'My soul is sorrowful to the point of death. Wait here and keep awake with me.'
(Matthew 26:36-8)

Try to imagine yourself present as Jesus leaves the last supper and makes his way to Gethsemane. How do you feel? What do you do?

When you arrive at the garden, Jesus draws aside into the shadows, to pray. He asks one or two friends to go with him. Where are you in the scene now?

Hear his words, out of the darkness: 'Stay with me ... Keep watch with me ...' How do you feel when you hear these words? How do you respond?

Can you remember any moments in your journey with God when you felt that you were being consecrated by him for a particular ministry or role in life? You may perhaps remember your Confirmation, or a time of spiritual renewal, or the growing awareness of a vocation, or the moments may have been very private, in times of prayer. Recall them now, before God. If you feel drawn to do so, perhaps renew the promises you made to God at those times and ask him to bless your continuing intention to follow him in those special ways.

❦

Do you know any 'starmakers'? Any people who have known a deep darkness in their lives, perhaps through pain or handicap, abuse or cruelty, loneliness or depression, and have in some way 'pierced the darkness', taking their personal pain through a spiritual barrier, and become a source of strength, encouragement or enlightenment for others? Give thanks for them now, to God. If you feel it is possible, or appropriate, to do so, you might like to find a way of letting them know (if they are still alive) how much you honour their courage.

❦

What burdens do you feel you are carrying in your life today that seem almost too heavy to bear? Name them to God in your prayer, and tell him honestly how you feel. Then try to bring your inner compass to stillness and ask God to hold your heart in the perfect balance of True North. While you are at that still centre of peace, take up the burden again and ask God to balance it across your shoulders in *his* way.

❦

Where is the worst area of pain in your life at present? Let it come into your awareness in prayer. Lay every feeling before God, without fear. This is your Gethsemane. Ask the Lord to stay with you, and to watch and pray with you. Ask him to draw your pain into his own. Read and pray through any of the Gospel accounts of Jesus' suffering, his trial, his torture and his death. In what parts do you feel closest to him? Why do you think this is?

How is his experience connecting to your own?

※

Make a conscious attempt to still yourself, when another person is stand-ing in front of you, and remember that the risen Lord is standing right behind them. Would that make a difference to your way of relating to them? Repeat the exercise whenever you have a chance, until it starts to become a habit. Try it especially when someone is being difficult, or is making demands on you, or is in need of your love in some particular way.

15. TO LOVE YOU MORE
DEARLY ...

What can I give him?

The *Spiritual Exercises* end with a contemplation which invites us to reflect on how we will respond to the immense love that God has shown to us, and with a prayer of personal surrender of the gift of our hearts and lives to the one who holds our lives in his own heart. Of course, your response to this question is a matter for your own heart alone. In this chapter I would only like to share a few of the challenges that have arisen from my own reflections about how it might be possible to begin to respond to God's gift of unconditional love.

Let me begin by introducing you to two friends of mine: let us call them Marjorie and Frank. Marjorie is a social worker. She has gone into this kind of work in later life. As a younger woman she brought up two children of her own, and two adopted children. These last two were both from deeply disturbed backgrounds and Marjorie and her husband Frank have given years and years of their lives to sheltering, nurturing and guiding these two seriously damaged young lives.

When she lost her job as a laboratory assistant, through redundancy, Marjorie went back to college, taking all her lived experience with her, in the hope that she might be able to make it fruitful for other people. She has finished her studies now, and is working day by day with troubled families and with those who are themselves adopting distressed children. This work often takes her into the courts, where she is sometimes called upon to give evidence as an 'expert witness'.

Expert evidence! Most of us would not see ourselves as likely to be called to be 'expert witnesses' in a court of law. Yet, listen to what St. Paul has to say:

'Life to me is not a thing to waste words on, provided that when I finish my race I have carried out the mission the Lord Jesus gave me – and that was to bear witness to the Good News of God's grace.'

(Acts 20:24)

We all know that we are called to 'witness' for our faith and our God. Most of us have, perhaps, a rather vague notion of what that might mean, and none of us can ever know in advance what it might cost. Marjorie's story may help a little. Being a witness means giving evidence. It means having that particular quality that reveals something of God to those around us. It means that the Godseed in our hearts has germinated and is showing some outward sign of life – in growth, in blossom, or in fruit. If our lives reveal no evidence of the God indwelling in our hearts, then we are no use as witnesses.

So what might it mean to be called as 'expert witnesses', as Marjorie is sometimes called upon to do?

The word 'expert' is related to several other words in our language. It is the past participle of the verb 'to experience'. An expert is *one who has experienced*. It comes from the Latin verb *'experior'* which means 'to try, prove, test, undertake, attempt, risk, undergo, experience, contend with'.

Of all these shades of meaning, perhaps the most telling, for our spiritual journey, is 'to risk'. When we take the risk of faith, we open ourselves up to the *experience* of God, and that experience is our proof, living and lived proof, of his reality and his power and his love – proof first to ourselves, and then to others, who begin to notice its effects on us.

It also has the same root as the word 'experiment'. An expert is *'one who has experimented, one who has tried things out, to test their truth and their reality'*.

And now, here in the last chapter of these explorations in Ignatian spirituality, is it not true to say that this is what we have been doing – not just in our sharing of these pages, but in our individual life and faith journeys over the years? We have been risking the exposure of our innermost being to God in prayer, and reflecting on that experience, and testing the truth of our own discernment in the light of how it affects our real daily lives.

If we look back now to the question *'What can I give him?'*, we can perhaps approach the answer in two ways. First, there is an answer that applies to all of us, and in which we can share, and help each other. Second, there is an answer that applies to each of us individually, and can only be fully known and given between each of us and God.

We could summarise these two answers like this:

I am called to be an expert witness for Christ in the court of his creation.
I am called to become fully who I most truly and eternally AM.

So what *can* I give him? ...

I can give him the evidence of my lived experience as a sign of his real and loving presence in his world.

And I can give him back – fulfilled – the dream he first had of me when he created me.

The first is a collective gift to God from all of us. The second is an individual gift which each of us must work out for ourselves, with God, in our prayer and in our living.

Giving expert evidence

What makes a witness into an expert witness? Well, in a nutshell, merely *witnessing* to God can be done just with words, and from the head, but *expert* witnesses reveal God out of their lived experience of him, and in the authority of his truth that they hold in their hearts.

There is a Latin expression '*experto crede*', which means 'You can take my word for it, because I have tried'. Can we apply this expression to our own belief in the reality of God in our lives and our world? As we consider this thought, it might be helpful to break it down into easier stages. Reflect for a few minutes on these more personal questions:

- Have I actually *tried* (experimented)? Have I tried walking with God through the ordinary events of my ordinary days? Have I tried noticing, each night, where, when, in whom I have especially sensed his presence? Have I tried tracking my own moods and noting when I felt close to God and when I felt far away? Have I tried listening to him, at a personal level, in my prayer and in his Word, and letting what I hear take root in how I live?

- If I have tried it, do I *trust* my own experience of God? When I feel him leading me in a particular direction, do I trust his reality sufficiently to risk following him? Remember the story of the man who entertained the crowds by pushing a wheelbarrow across a tightrope drawn across a gaping chasm. 'Do you believe I can do it?' he asked them. 'Of course we do,' they shouted. 'Who will get in the wheelbarrow then?' he invited. And they all fell silent. Do I merely *believe* that God holds my life in his hands, or do I *trust* his guiding in my living of it?

- If I trust my own experience of God, do I have the courage to stand up and *show* that trust, even when that means swimming against the flow? Standing up to be counted doesn't, I feel, mean, primarily, standing up and proclaiming our faith in words to reluctant bystanders (though it might do!). Marjorie and Frank, for example, are committed Christians, and they know that Christ is the source of all the power and the love in their lives, but they don't tell people this unless they are asked. There is no need. It would be like giving a botany lecture while standing under a cherry tree in the full glory of its blossom, beneath a blue May sky. The reality is so much more eloquent and potent than the mere scientific facts. Marjorie and Frank's lives blossom and fruit with the life of their Lord and that is what gives such force and authority to their 'expert evidence'.

Lived experience speaks for itself!

Three questions, then, to consider: *Have I tried it? Do I trust it? Will I let it show?*

Giving back the dream

We began this journey of exploration by reflecting on who we most truly *are*, at the heart of ourselves, where the Godseed is implanted. It is here, in the 'who' that God's dream for us is unfolding. Our lives are the space in which that dream takes shape, and our gift to our God is his dream fulfilled.

We have seen something of what it might mean to become co-creators in God's dream for us. We have seen how we first need to recognise that heart of ourselves, where God is, incarnate in each of us as he was incarnate in his Son, who called us his brothers and sisters. We have also observed that we are free to direct our lives either 'home' towards our God-centre, or out and away from it. Then come our fears, and our false images of God, that obstruct the dream's unfolding, and our deepest desires, that nourish it and show us something of its ultimate shape and beauty. And our addictions and attachments that divert our energy away from the unfolding of our deepest desire.

God's dream in our hearts is a tender, but all-powerful seed. We are charged with the task of bringing the dream to birth. How can we do that? Ignatius suggests a way that leads, through prayer, to an ever-deepening intimacy with the Lord, in his earthly ministry, in his Passion and in his resurrected life. Day by day, prayer by prayer, lived moment by lived moment, we notice and respond to the constant encounters with the living God, and every time we do so, our roots are strengthened, and the Godseed grows a little stronger towards the unique manifestation of its creator, that it is going to become.

There is no great mystery surrounding this process. It can all be expressed very simply. Our increasing intimacy with God will inevitably foster the desire in us to become the person he is dreaming us to be, and when that is our deepest desire, that will be what, eternally, IS. By surrendering the lesser desires of our lives, and submitting to whatever kind of 'dying' that entails, we will cross the threshold of resurrection, just as he promised we would.

Towards the end of his *Exercises*, Ignatius invites us to reflect again on all the ways in which God has revealed his overflowing love to us, personally, and in community. We are being drawn, through our own deepest desires, back into the perfect love-union that is expressed by the Trinity. In a very real way this is the centre of our being, to which our inner journey is destined.

We began by reflecting on our journey to the truest heart of ourselves, where God is indwelling, and then out again, carrying the transforming treasure from the centre to the outermost edges of our lives. Now we can

Giving back the dream ...

see this movement on a much larger scale, as a journey into the heart of the Trinity, where each Person is in perfect inter-relationship with, and inter-dependent on, the others.

This relationship is the circle of eternal joy in which God so rejoices that he calls us to share it eternally with him. In fact, he calls each of us, individually, to become the fourth person of the Trinity. But he calls us not just for ourselves, but, because the Trinity is the divine model for human community, he asks us, and empowers us to carry the transforming experience back to our still-untransformed world, until our human community becomes His Kingdom.

Carrying God in a bottomless bucket

Carrying God to the world sounds like a tall order – and if we think we can really do that, we may be teetering on the brink of a Messiah complex!

There was a time when I used to think that we could receive grace from God into our own 'containers', rather like the old days when people used to take their jugs and jars out to the milk-cart to get their daily supply of milk. How much you got depended on the size of your container. When it came to grace, I thought, I would receive as much as my heart would hold, and if I hoped for more, I would have to do something about 'expanding' my heart. This way of looking at things served me reasonably well for a while (even though, as you can see, it is rather a *me*-centred approach to the problem) – until, that is, the bottom fell out of my bucket.

Maybe there have been times in *your* life, when your 'system' packed in, and your tried and tested methods of doing things just didn't seem to work any more. Maybe it was some traumatic experience that brought you to a fuller realisation of your own inability to save even yourself, let alone the rest of the world. Or maybe it was just the gradual advance of a sense of personal helplessness, when it came to questions arising out of your journey with God. Whatever it was, it quite possibly left you feeling as though your solid certainties had become unreliable, and the jug you had been using to collect your 'daily grace' from the milk-float of your prayer, had sprung a leak.

Every life is shot through with little 'dyings'. At the time they seem only to diminish us, but *over time*, if we look back reflectively, they may become the very moments when we really came alive. The bucket becomes a pipe.

The few litres of grace we might have held in our bucket turn into the *possibility* of a constant stream that – at last – is free to flow through our open-ended hearts.

Channels of grace...

are often made out of bottomless buckets!

We can no longer bracket ourselves with neat beginnings and endings, and when God removes our brackets and leaves us feeling naked and bereft, he is actually throwing open our limiting barriers and exposing us to the pain and the glory of eternity. Pain, because we cannot bear, lightly, the truth that we are not ourselves the purpose of it all, but the provisional containers *through* which the Purpose flows; and glory, because that Purpose is so infinitely greater than anything our blinkered hearts could ever have imagined.

Once the ends are off our life's pipeline, and the certainties we thought we held are dissolved in the acid of experience, grace *can* flow, freely. Or not so freely? For myself, honesty demands that I acknowledge the many blockages and resistances that cling to the walls of my own heart's channel, like limpets to a boat's hull. Detaching the limpets is painful. Yet even here, there is great promise: the more freely grace flows, the more clear the channel becomes. What begins as the merest trickle will swell, and the more power it gathers, the more surely will it remove my barnacles.

I cannot give God to the world. Only God himself can do that. But I *can* give him some space, and if space is what I seek, where might I find it if not in my own inner emptiness? In those places that hurt me so much that I try to fill them up with achievements and attachments. When I learn to let go of those false friends, then space is something I find I have plenty of. I can give God my empty, broken bucket, to be a little segment in a channel for his peace.

Catacombs or honeycombs?

We all know the rhyme about the two men who looked out from prison bars, and the one saw mud, the other stars. It can sound all so easy, and we know, too well, that the stars are not always in evidence. Some of the explorations in this book have underlined the possibilities of reflecting on our own experience, day by day, to discover where God has been in them – to discover, as it were, the golden threads of meaning, truth and joy that run through our days. We have also become aware of the extent to which we choose our own destinies, by choosing how to respond to the 'given-ness' of our lives – in terms of the circles, we respond to our circumstances in the HOW circle, and how we respond makes us see the WHERE in new ways. These new ways, in turn, gradually shape and transform our WHO.

Suppose we were left – as well we may be, on the other side of death's mystery – with only our WHO to bring home to God, what would it look like? When we come into the fullness of God's presence, what will we be holding in our hands? A honeycomb, or a catacomb?

Whichever it is, it will have been formed out of the many cells of our every-days. Every time we look out of the prison bars and see the mud, every time we fall asleep recalling only the irritations and problems of the day, every time we look into the face of our neighbour and see the faults, we have sealed another grave-chamber for the death of our Godseed. Every time we look out from our constraints and shackles and see a star, every time we look back over a day and see a moment's joy, every time we look into our neighbour's eyes and see the love inside him, we open up a cell of sweetness for the delight of our own hearts and the world's.

It seems to me to matter, very much, how we choose, because in every moment we are either condemning the world, and ourselves, to a little bit more death, or releasing it to a little bit more of life.

The bees create honeycombs unconsciously, in the course of simply fulfilling their own deepest desire. We might, in our prayer, ask God for the grace to do likewise.

Knitting squares for the Kingdom blanket

When I was little, ham-fisted and left-handed (now I am large, ham-fisted and still left-handed!), my aunt used to try, very patiently, to teach me to knit. Eventually, after a titanic struggle, I learned to knit my way across the rows, and even managed to produce a few knitted squares to contribute to the 'refugee blankets' we used to make in those days. But I always needed my aunt's help to cast on and cast off. Those operations remained mysteries beyond my comprehension.

All this arose for me again one day in prayer, and I could see the stitches in my square as a sort of parable of the events and relationships in my life. Every stitch was an essential and unique part of the fabric of my 'square'. God 'cast me on' to the needles of my own particular circumstances, when I was conceived, and gradually, painstakingly, I learned to form my stitches. Sometimes I got them wrong – too tight or too loose – sometimes I dropped them completely and had to live with the hole. Sometimes I tore into the wool with my needles, and made myself – or others – bleed. Sometimes I glowed with pride as a row was successfully completed. Sometimes I wept with frustration. Sometimes I wanted to tear the whole thing apart and start again, with different wool, on different needles.

I'm still knitting ... but I have a friend who is dying. As he makes the longest journey, from life to Life, he is surrounded by his memories. His room is graced, really *graced*, with rows of fine stitches: photographs of people who have been significant to him; poems and meditations; icons and gifts he has treasured; music that has inspired him; the books he has written, the children he has fathered, the wife he has loved. Substantial memories, and dreams worth the keeping.

His wool is almost worked. Soon he will be bringing the square of his life to his God. In these months I have had the unimaginable privilege of standing alongside as he and God have been casting off ...

One by one he surrenders his stitches. The process is bitter-sweet, shot through with pangs of grief and heartbreak, yet transfigured by the promise of that which is being completed.

I know that soon he will hear the words of heaven: '*Consummatum est*'. 'It is completed. The square I gave you to knit is finished.' Perhaps he asks himself, as I do when I look to my own casting-off, 'Will the Lord accept the square I bring him for the Kingdom blanket?'

And I think then, that it isn't going to matter so much about the mistakes, and the spoiled patterns, and the dropped stitches. What is going to matter is the one crucial question: 'Does it help to keep my people warm?'

A blanket full of faults and holes
to keep you warm,

or the perfect masterpiece
that I never made?

※

My friend tells me that now, when he passes the shelf of books that he has written, they seem to whisper to him: 'Now, *live* what you have written.' I pass those whispered words on to you. 'Now, let us *live* what we have discovered.'

A prayer of surrender

Ignatius made this his prayer of surrender. It is not a prayer to be made lightly. God may answer it in ways you do not expect and cannot predict:

Take, Lord, and receive
my liberty,
my memory,
my understanding,
my entire will,
everything I have and call my own.
You gave me all these gifts,
and to you I return them.
Dispose of them entirely according to your will.
Give me only your love and your grace.
That is all I ask.

Here is my personal interpretation. It is inspired by Hannah's surrender of her longed-for child, Samuel. Her deepest desire has been fulfilled in Samuel's birth, and she responds by recognising her even deeper desire to offer what she most cherishes to the Lord. She makes Samuel over to the Lord. You might like to reflect on how your own deep desires are being fulfilled, and how far you feel able to surrender the treasure of your heart into the hands and the authority of God. Use this prayer if it helps you, or perhaps you would like to formulate your own.

Take and Receive

'This is the child I prayed for, and the Lord granted me what I asked him.
Now I make him over to the Lord for the whole of his life.
He is made over to the Lord. There she left him, for the Lord.'
(1 Samuel 1:27–8)

I place myself into your hands, Lord. Take me and receive me. Take me, for I am yours. Receive me, for I give myself freely to you.

I place into your hands, my liberty.
It sets me free to love and to serve. It gives me the great gifts of choice and self-determination. But it tempts me into choosing the lesser good, the

lesser gods. It leaves me free to choose for myself, instead of for love. It beguiles me into believing only in myself. It allows me to choose to do harm, to destroy and to die.

Take, receive my liberty under your leadership.

It is made over to the Lord.

I place into your hands, my memory.

It draws me back to times and places past, where I have known your touch upon my life. It leads me through my history to your mystery. But it holds in its power all my 'if only's. It tangles its brambles round my heart, fixing me in past hurts and harms, causing me to look back and turn to salt, corrosive with resentment. It holds me unforgiven in past wrongs that you have healed. It darkens my hopes with regrets.

Take, receive my memory under your leadership.

It is made over to the Lord.

I place into your hands, my understanding.

It leads me more deeply into your Truth, but it binds me in the narrow spaces of my own little truths. It gives me insight to help me understand the way others respond to life. It gives me the words and the structures to express my own responses. But it tempts me into settling for human understanding, when you are calling my soul towards the divine. It lures me into the cul-de-sac of pride and self-satisfaction, when I want to be satisfied with nothing less than you.

Take, receive my understanding under your leadership.

It is made over to the Lord.

I place into your hands, my imagination.

It carries me to the heavens, as a firework bursts across the night sky. It leads me into heart-knowledge, spanning time and space to make all things present. It kindles the flame of your Truth in the darkness of my own mind. But it also feeds my fears. It seduces truth into fantasy and caution into dread. It opens up the gateway to your Reality, or it traps me in the self-imposed enclosures of my own make-believe.

Take, receive my imagination under your leadership.

It is made over to the Lord.

I place into your hands, my power to feel.
My feelings draw me into the depth and joy of love. They invite my life-stream to pour into yours. They open my arms and my heart and unlock my griefs and my longings. But they also suck me down the spirals of bitterness and despair and hold me captive to my passing moods. They are a candle, warm with love-light, or the destructive sweep of a forest fire.
Take, receive my feelings under your leadership.
They are made over to the Lord.

I place into your hands, my entire will.
Once, when time began, it was in harmony with yours. But sin fragmented your creation, and every creature took hold of its own little world and ruled according to its own narrow will. I want it to be otherwise, but my wanting achieves nothing, because my will remains stubbornly my own.
Take, receive my entire will under your leadership.
It is made over to the Lord.

You have given me these precious gifts, Lord, the first-born fruits of the love that flows between us. And to you, Lord, to your loving leadership, I return them. You are their author, and I commit them into your authority. Do with them as you will.
They are made over to the Lord.

Give me only your love, and your grace, for that is all I need. Then I, too, shall be made over to the Lord.

15: TO LOVE YOU MORE DEARLY ...
Suggestions for prayer and reflection

Six days before the Passover, Jesus went to Bethany, where Lazarus was, whom he had raised from the dead. They gave a dinner for him there; Martha waited on them and Lazarus was among those at table. Mary brought in a pound of very costly ointment, pure nard, and with it anointed the feet of Jesus, wiping them with her hair; the house was full of the scent of the ointment.

(John 12:1-3)

Imagine that you are in the house of Mary, Martha and Lazarus, when Jesus arrives to spend the evening with you. The brother and two sisters are all present to Jesus in quite different ways, in this story, each according to his or her personality. How will *you* respond to the Lord, during this meeting? What will be *your* particular way of showing your love for him? In your prayer, let yourself respond to him in whatever way you feel drawn to do. How does he react to your gift of love? How do you feel about the gifts that others are giving him? How do you feel as you make your gift to him? Speak to him, and tell him of your feelings. Listen to him, as he tells you his.

※

Suppose you were asked to be an 'expert witness' to the reality of God in your own life. What parts of your lived experience do you feel especially reveal the power and love of God, to yourself, and to others? In which areas of your life do you feel able to say to others 'God is real, God is love, God is power. You can take my word for it, because I have tried.'

※

When you give God the dream that your life has grown out of his Godseed in your heart, how do you think you might describe that unique fulfilment that is yours, and yours alone, to discover? What characteristics will it have? What will be its special beauties and properties? What is God growing in your heart, even now, that is going to be 'a dream worth the keeping'? Don't be shy about your God-dream. You are only giving God back the fulfilment of what he has first given to you. You are giving him of his own. Give it joyfully, without false modesty.

※

Have there been any times when the bottom has fallen out of your 'bucket'? With hindsight, can you see that any of those times have become times of grace? If so, give thanks to God for them in your prayer, and ask him to turn your trickle into his abundant flow.

※

Where are the empty spaces in your heart? Is there loneliness, disappointment, heartache, grief? Do you feel able to make that emptiness over to God, as a space for him to fill with grace, for you and for others? Are you aware of any blockages in your channels, caused by the things with which you have tried to fill up your emptiness?

※

Reflect back over the past twenty-four hours. Every minute has been potentially contributing to death or to life – building a catacomb or a honeycomb. Which parts of today have been contributing to the burial of your Godseed, and which have been helping to bring it to life and growth?

※

Imagine your life as a knitted square. Can you see the parts where you 'dropped your stitches' and lost your pattern? Now feel the warmth of the wool between your fingers. Which do you think is more important to the refugee who will use your blanket – its accuracy or its warmth? Let yourself cherish each stitch, as a unique event or relationship in your life. Value it, and thank God for it, *as it is*, not for what it might have been.

※

Reflect on the 'Prayer of Surrender' on page 242. If you feel drawn to do so, write your own version of it, bringing to God the gifts of your being, and asking him to receive them into his authority, for he is indeed their author and their source.

BENEDICTUS

We began this journey by smiling over Wainwright's instruction to 'turn left at the third hawthorn tree'. It was a landmark pregnant with invitation. Which was fine if you were standing at the beginning of the path, map in hand, ready to notice all the right landmarks and make all the best possible turnings to lead you home to your deepest desire . . .

. . . But most of us don't start the journey at the beginning, or even at any other sensible, prescribed point. We begin, quite simply, from where we are, and for most of us that will be long after we have already *missed* the third hawthorn tree and perhaps a good few other apparently vital land-marks. I am reminded of the traveller who lost his way and asked for directions. After a long and convoluted explanation of how to reach his destination, his informant gave up, with the comment 'But if I were you I wouldn't start from here.'

God knows better. With God we always start exactly where we are and nowhere else, and he is both the path and the compass. So it becomes possible to stop for a moment, on the journey, and look back at the maze of paths behind us. Like most of you, perhaps, I can now see several hawthorn trees where I took the wrong turning. In Ignatius' language, I made the wrong 'election'. So what to do about it now? Stand and regret? . . . Or go back to the bottom of the hill and try again . . . Or remember that God is Now and God is Here, wherever we are, in whatever unchosen places or situations, and that it is *God* whom we seek, not a particular path.

I remember at school singing the hymn 'God is working his purpose out, as year succeeds to year'. At the time I suspected that this was wishful thinking, or that, if it was true, this purpose would always be a mystery to me. I know better now. I know that my own deepest desires are gradually drawing me closer to God's desire for me. I can look back now over a fair length of my own path, and see some of the other paths I might have taken. Some of them may seem (from here) to have offered an easier, more direct route home, but I can never, shall never, need never know what pitfalls they might have been concealing. All I need to know is that wherever I am is where I am with God, in the here and now, and that this journey, which is my real 'vocation', is unfolding itself out of all my life's choices – wise and unwise – as a skilled weaver might create his cloth out of all kinds of unlikely bits of wool.

Indeed, God being Who-He-IS, he gives his special blessing upon those very places where we ourselves feel most vulnerable and broken and lost. Let us share that blessing now, free of regret for the landmarks we have missed, alert and alive with trust for all that lies ahead . . .

'I bless the poverty in your heart, that knows its own emptiness, because that gives me space to grow my Kingdom there.'

'I bless that in you that touches others gently, because everyone responds to gentleness, and gentleness can capture even hardened hearts.'

'I bless that in you which grieves and aches for all that is lost or can never be, because that is my opportunity to comfort you with my, much greater, love.'

'I bless that in you which longs and strives after your own deepest truth and after truth for the world, because even as you pray, I am constantly satisfying these deep unspoken longings.'

'I bless you every time you show mercy and forgiveness, because that is like a little window in your heart, setting you free from resentment and opening up a space for me to enter and to heal.'

'I bless the purity of your heart, because that is the elusive centre where your deepest desire meets mine. That is where we meet face to face.'

'I bless the peacemaker in you, that in you which seeks the peace that passes understanding, knowing the cost of its obtaining, because that is what I sent my Son to give, and in your peacemaking you become my daughter.'

'I bless even those things in your experience of journeying with me that feel like persecution and abuse and misunderstanding, because they are the proof that your faith is no illusion.'

These, Lord, surely, are your original blessings, that precede, and supersede, my original sin, and assure me that your joy, your peace, your love are so much larger than my fearing and my failing. Yes, this *is* the Gospel of the Lord.

WHERE you are (however unchosen)
is the place of blessing

HOW you are (however broken)
is the place of grace

WHO you are, in your Becoming
is your place in the Kingdom